75 1.60

D1437563

Philosophy

AND ITS

History

HAROLD R. SMART

Emeritus Professor of Philosophy
Cornell University

THE OPEN COURT PUBLISHING COMPANY 1962
ESTABLISHED 1887 LA SALLE, ILLINOIS

Library of Congress Catalog Card Number: 62-9573

PHILOSOPHY AND ITS HISTORY

To *F. G. S.*

PREFACE

Courses in the history of philosophy are a generally recognized part of a college curriculum. Such courses admirably serve the general purposes of a humane education, exposing the student, as they do, to the most general ideas and the loftiest thoughts of the greatest thinkers of all times and places. They "broaden the mind," render it receptive to new ideas, and in general, stimulate and foster genuine concern for all cultural values.

True, the bewildering diversity of philosophical theories and systems which history reveals, may be temporarily unsettling to the youthful mind; but in the end the healthy lesson to take all such theories with a grain of salt, usually prevails; and, for the rest, the original impact of those theories will in the course of time be largely modulated anyhow.

It rarely happens, in this context, that a potentially embarrassing question is raised, or, if raised, answered, in other than the vaguest possible terms, by professional teachers of philosophy. But it is to this very question, which is really of basic importance to the serious student of philosophy, that the following study addresses itself. This is the question as to the intrinsic significance, for philosophy as such, of its history.

The fact that up to the present time comparatively few philosophers have given much thought to attempts to answer this question makes it possible to include in a rather brief study such as this, practically all of the principal answers which have so far been proposed, and to examine those answers with a view to composing a way of reading the history of philosophy that seems, in the light of the examination, to be the most reasonable and pregnant one.

West Acton, Mass.,
August 10, 1962

ACKNOWLEDGMENTS

The author wishes to thank the following publishers for their permission to quote from their works, as specifically noted in the text:

Bookman Associates, New York, for *Dilthey's Philosophy of Existence,* by Kluback and Weinbaum.

The Clarendon Press, Oxford, for *Collingwood's Idea of History,* by T. M. Knox (Editor); and also *Autobiography,* and *Essay on Metaphysics,* both by R. G. Collingwood.

Harcourt, Brace & Co., New York, for *History: Its Theory and Practice,* by B. Croce (transl. Ainslee).

Macmillan & Co., London, for *Logic,* by B. Croce (transl. Ainslee).

Meridian Books, New York, for *Existentialism from Dostoevsky to Sartre,* edited by W. Kaufmann.

Philosophical Library, New York, for *Bergson's The Creative Mind* (transl. M. Andison).

R. Piper & Co., Verlag, Munich, for *Die Grossen Philosophen,* by Karl Jaspers.

Presses Universitaires de France, Paris, for *Historie de la Philosophie,* by E. Bréhier.

Routledge & Kegan Paul, London, for *William Dilthey, An Introduction,* by H. A. Hodges.

Charles Scribner's Sons, New York, for *The Unity of Philosophical Experience,* by E. Gilson.

The University of North Carolina Press, Chapel Hill, N. C., for *Wilhelm Dilthey's The Essence of Philosophy* (transl. Emery & Emery).

TABLE OF CONTENTS

CHAPTER   PAGE

PREFACE vii

1. INTRODUCTORY: ECLECTICISM—
   TOWARD A HISTORY OF
   PHILOSOPHY 1

2. COMTE AND HEGEL: DEVELOPMENT ... 18

3. RENOUVIER AND DILTHEY: THE
   CLASSIFICATION OF PHILOSOPHICAL
   SYSTEMS 30

4. CROCE AND COLLINGWOOD: THE
   IDENTIFICATION OF PHILOSOPHY
   WITH HISTORY 62

5. KARL JASPERS: THE GREAT THINKERS. 85

6. BERGSON, GILSON, AND RUSSELL:
   INTUITION AND DOGMATISM 114

7. CONCLUSION: THE DIALECTICAL
   NATURE OF PHILOSOPHY AND ITS
   HISTORY 128

   NOTES 151

   INDEX OF NAMES....................155

   INDEX OF SUBJECTS.................157

Philosophy

AND ITS

History

1. *INTRODUCTORY:* ECLECTICISM— TOWARD A HISTORY OF PHILOSOPHY

Among other noteworthy features of the Renaissance is the appearance of the first tentative gropings toward a history of philosophy. These gropings consist of compilations, after the manner of such ancient writers as Plutarch, Sextus Empiricus, Stobaeus, and above all Diogenes Laertius, of the views and opinions of various sects, of accounts of the "Lives" of certain thinkers, and of more or less inaccurate versions and translations of greater or lesser portions of the original works of ancient thinkers.

Although there was as yet no real comprehension of history as history, of the possible significance for philosophy of its own history, this tentative and widespread prying into the past, as it might be called, did at least reveal the existence of diverse ancient sects and of a temporal succession of schools, thus affording material for a new kind of learning, and for the consequent development of scepticism and eclecticism.

In his *Advancement of Learning,*[1] for example, Sir Francis Bacon conceives of the history of philosophy mainly as the history of sects, including the most famous controversies which have occupied the learned of all the diverse schools. It was quite in this spirit that George Horn wrote what perhaps may be described as the first general history of philosophy—*Historiae philosophicae libri septem, quibus de origine successione, sectio et vita philosophorum ab orbe conditio ad nostram aetatem agitur* (1645).

The authors of such works attempted in a sense to bring back the past, rather than simply to inform themselves of it in a properly historical way. Thus only an author who was himself a Platonist would write a history of Platonism, and the same is true of Stoicism, Epicureanism, etc. One of the most important of these schools or sects is, of course, Scepticism; for one of the traditional arguments for that line of thought bases itself upon the existence of this very diversity of sects.[2]

In other words, the net result of such a way of dealing with the thought of the past is naturally enough its fragmentation into an indefinite number of contending doctrines, among which the individual thinker either casts his choice in accordance with his own personal intellectual inclinations; or, seeing that one line of thought, turn and turn about, appears to negate all of the others, such a thinker eventually embraces scepticism.

To the creative thinkers of the seventeenth century, it appeared that the only way of escape from such a fatality was to break philosophy free from philology, from the verbiage that had clouded the minds and distorted the ideas of the thinkers of the past. In this sense, to be a philosopher is to be anti-historical, is radically to break with the past, and is to begin anew, on a new foundation. As the historian Horn himself observed, his century, among whose shining lights are Descartes and Hobbes, is the century of the philosopher, while the preceding age had belonged to the philologists. The basic problem of Descartes and Hobbes, accordingly, was to find, above and beyond the opinions of the sects, the sources of the one true philosophy, sources to be found in the nature of the human mind itself.

From this point of view, obviously, the history of philosophy becomes merely an enumeration or record of errors and aberrations, a sort of museum of the divagations of thought in its journey through the ages.

J. J. Brücker's *Historia critica philosophiae a mundus incunabilis,*[3] a work which enjoyed the favor of the encyclopedists, for example, takes its cue from St. Augustine's *City of God.* According to Brücker, philosophy has a divine origin and is as old as the world itself. The Greeks therefore misled later thinkers in holding that they were the first philosophers. Actually, the Greeks borrowed their doctrines from Moses and other Jewish patriarchs, and from Egypt, Babylonia, India, etc. In assembling and partly digesting these traditions, the Greeks caused them to degenerate into various sects, and either into scepticism, which spells the end of philosophy, or into neo-Platonism, which is a corruption of Christian philosophy. In short, the history of philosophy is but the melancholy record of the gradual and progressive decadence of the human mind. From as far back as the days of the church fathers, and as far into modern times as the Age of Voltaire, this theory of the decadence of philosophical thought with the passage of time was rather widespread. In his *Traité des Systèmes,* for example, Condillac (1715–80) disparagingly describes even the works of early modern philosophers as products of "the imagination."

Such, up to, and during part of the eighteenth century, is the judgment of philosophy, framed in the light of its new conception of itself, upon its own past. Or should this statement be reversed, to the effect that it was in part due to the inability of thinkers of those times to find any positive meaning in the diversity of philosophical theories, as recorded by the historians, that those same thinkers sought so persistently for a refuge which they professed to find either in a set of indubitable truths beyond the reach of temporal vicissitudes and human idiosyncracies, or in some permanent, sheerly factual traits of human nature? What is more spontaneously and naively natural, as a first reaction to the disagreements and conflicts of the schools, as revealed by the historian's pioneering labors, than a profound intellectual and moral *malaise,* and a consequent heroic endeavor to overcome, once and for all, what, under the circumstances, could only be deemed a fatal weakness infecting all past philosophizing?

There is good reason, and considerable indirect evidence, that such considerations did indeed exert an influence, if mainly unconsciously, upon the philosophical thinking of the seventeenth and eighteenth centuries. And how natural, if not inevitable, too, that in their search for certainty, philosophers, like their colleagues, the brilliantly successful natural scientists, should turn their backs to the past, and look to the sciences themselves for inspiration and positive guidance!

II

Meanwhile, from the seventeenth century on, new conceptions of the history of philosophy and new perspectives for interpreting and evaluating the past, were first emerging and then being gradually developed by the historians themselves. In spite of the apparent surface diversity of the various schools and sects, historians were beginning to search for, and claiming to have found substantial evidence of a real underlying unity of philosophical thought.

In his *Conciliator Philosophicus* (1609), Goclenius already foreshadows this tendency. In that work the author first painstakingly classified the contradictory doctrines of the various sects on each subject, and then proceeded to resolve these contradictions by professing to show that they were only apparent and not real. *Syncretism* was the name given to this new and tentatively positive historical procedure, and, as affirming the basic accord of philosophical thought with itself under all of its superficially contradictory manifestations, it was already regarded by the historian, Horn, as the real outcome of the history of philosophy.

Tending in the same general direction, though with a significant difference, was the doctrine which came to be described as *Eclecticism*. Lipsius (1585) already writes in praise of "the eclectic sect which reads attentively and chooses judicially"; other works of the same tenor are those by J. C. Sturm: *Philosophia eclectica* (1686), and *Physica eclectica* (1697 ff.). And in his famous *Encyclopédie,* Diderot gives his approval to the same doctrine. Eclecticism, he avers, dares to think for itself, and, out of all the various philosophies which it analyzes, impartially constructs one of its own. Thus the history of the contending schools becomes a means of freeing oneself from them.

A little later, Deslandes even went so far as to protest against the very idea of a history of sects, as such. Such a way of understanding history is uninstructive, and conceals the underlying continuity in and through all the surface diversity. The correct procedure is to trace the principal theories to their sources, and, in the process of noting their infinite variety, to discover the well-nigh imperceptible but significant interconnections, the delicate *liaisons,* between them. Thus will come to light the circumstances under which these theories were engendered, one after the other, and frequently the ones *from* the others. The result will be a true appreciation of the ancient philosophers, and the realization that they really could not have thought and written other than they did.

But no doubt the most famous Conciliator of them all was none other than the great Leibniz. "Leibniz ist eine konziliatorische Natur," is the way Windelband describes him in his *Geschichte der Neueren Philosophie.*[4] While not a professed eclectic, Leibniz's encyclopedic mind constantly strove to mediate between, and to reconcile both the practical and the theoretical differences dividing churchmen, politicians, and thinkers from each other. Thus he contributed mightily to the spirit animating such historians of philosophy as were striving to find a positive meaning and value in even the seemingly most discordant theories of the past.

On the other hand, Reinhold (1758–1823) severely criticized the *Popular-philosophen* of his time who called themselves eclectics. "The formula: 'This proposition is affirmed by the common-sense of mankind' has become in our day, the first principle of a so-called new philosophy known as eclecticism." Aside from this principle, he continued, its adepts agree on nothing, each individual claiming the right to extract from all possible systems whatever *he* holds is in conformity with this common-sense, for which he quickly substitutes his own.[5]

In spite of its critics, however, eclecticism continued to attract certain advocates of this way of reading the history of philosophy well into the nineteenth century. Indeed it may be said to have reached its high point only with the famous lectures and writings on the history of philosophy by Victor Cousin (1792–1867). He based his interpretation of that history upon the following principles: (1) There exists in every human being a power or sense for truth, real and infallible. As contrasted with temporary, historical or scientific truth, this sense for truth is eternal and philosophical. It may be variously called reason, consciousness, or common sense, the human spirit, or thought. This philosophical truth is a latent power in mankind, often hidden, under ordinary circumstances, from conscious recognition. (2) Philosophical thinking is the art of bringing to clear consciousness a fragment of the whole truth, but due to human weaknesses this art exhausts itself in the course of its efforts, and seeks as it were to hide its defects by clothing itself in a system. (3) Thus truth exists at the present time in two forms: (a) hidden, virtual and subconsciously in the common sense which all men share; (b) in a clear and orderly form, but dispersed throughout the history of philosophy. (4) One method alone will lead to its discovery; i.e., history, judged and evaluated by common sense, will reveal a residue which will be the truth clearly and consciously realized.[6]

In his preface to *Philosophical Fragments*[7] Cousin further expands his "general views on the history of philosophy." He acutely observes, what more recent thinkers have too often overlooked, that some interpretations of the history of philosophy, based upon the claim by the historian to have in his possession the truth itself, in the form of a single basic principle of all truth, are compelled, in order to be consistent with themselves, to deny the truth to all past systems, save only those which have to some degree anticipated that principle, and implicitly at least rest upon it. And he goes on to remark that such an interpretation "is the final sentence" upon the historian's own system; "for it is a melancholy wisdom which has universal folly for its condition"; and "to defend ourselves only by accusing everybody else is to accuse and condemn ourselves." On the other hand, Eclecticism "can be applied with singular facility to history." Instead of proscribing all systems in order to justify itself, "it is satisfied with disengaging the inevitable portion of error that is mixed with the portion of truth." By invariably pursuing this course, as well with "enemies with their contrary errors," as with friends with their portions of truth, all thinkers become "friends and brothers," and out of the truths which they contribute, "purified and reconciled," there emerges "a vast whole, adequate to the expression of complete and universal truth."

But by what criterion is one to separate the wheat from the chaff, in accordance with this so laudable aim? Unfortunately Cousin's answer to this crucial question is far from satisfactory, and only serves to condemn his whole procedure out of his own mouth. Eclecticism, he asserts,

> supposes a system which serves it as a point of departure and a principle in the labyrinth of history; it demands as an instrument a rigid criticism . . . ; it has for its primary result the decomposition of all systems . . . , and for its final result their reconstruction in a new system which is the complete representation of consciousness in history.

In short, eclecticism

> begins with a philosophy, and proceeds by means of history, to the living demonstration of that philosophy . . . , illustrating the history of philosophy by this system and demonstrating this system by the whole history of philosophy.

Is it not obvious, upon reflection, that Cousin fails to take to heart his own criticism of other historians, save only that he, unlike those others, is professedly ready to recognize the truth wherever he finds it, instead of reserving that claim for his own thought alone? But this turns out to be a verbal distinction without a real difference; for, after all, the decision is exclusively Cousin's own as to what is true and what is false in preceding philosophies; the criteria are in his hands, and in his hands alone, quite as in the case of those historians whom he (rightly) castigates.

Or, to put the same point in other words, what guarantee is there that two philosophers, two professed eclectics, however faithfully following Cousin's prescription, would reach the same conclusions, and read the history of philosophy in essentially the same way? So vast is the material to be mastered and digested, so multifarious are the interpretations and emphases, that can plausibly be accorded to this system of thought and the other, that only by a miracle could one expect substantial agreement as to what was false and what was true, in this way. However laudable as an ideal, the impossibility of its realization in practice cannot but lead to its final rejection as a solution to the problem in question.

Even though it may seem to later thinkers that such strictures as those of Reinhold against eclecticism and its weaker sister syncretism, are fully justifiable, and might even be augmented, it cannot be denied that those ways of interpreting the history of philosophy powerfully stimulated a new interest in the subject. Instead of completely ignoring what might be called the historical dimension of philosophy, or, worse yet, of dismissing the philosophical systems of the past as so many false and barren doctrines, as glaring examples of how *not* to think, philosophers now found themselves squarely confronted with a question they could no longer evade. That philosophy does have a history could no longer be denied. The only question is, as to the way in which that history is to be understood in relation to one's own intellectual endeavors. In other words, the question of the meaning, the import, of its history, for philosophy itself, had henceforth to be squarely faced.

In a very real sense, indeed, this is only a part of another question, or only one question among others, concerning history in general. For history has now extended its sway over all human activities, and there are as many histories as there are significant differentiations among those activities and interests. In short, man may perhaps be less appropriately described as a rational animal, than as the animal that has a history. So that one further question, among others, that naturally arises is, what are the specific differentia of the history of philosophy, as compared and contrasted with all the other specialized histories of all the other significant activities that occupy men's minds and bodies, and upon which mankind expends its immensely various energies?

Further questions continuously arise, not singly but in clouds, to complicate and obscure what seemed to be, in the first instance, a relatively clear and simple matter—questions with which the

greatest minds have been wrestling now for generations with only relatively slight success.

And while it is far beyond the scope of such a
study as this even to frame many of these questions,
let alone proposing answers to them, it is surely
evident that no philosopher can do his own special
work in total disregard of them. Above all, he is
bound to carry on his own speculations, his own
theorizing, in the full light of the history of his own
species of intellectual activity. Whatever his major
interests in philosophy may be, and however completely he may profess to ignore or brush aside as
irrelevant, considerations of a historical sort, inevitably the future will see to it that "the verdict of
history" will embrace him and all his works in its
inescapable judgments.

III

However that may be, the moderate stimulus
given by eclecticism to a general interest in the history of philosophy, as distinguished from histories
of the various schools or sects, found powerful support in the belief in Progress which became one
of the leading characteristics of the late eighteenth
and early nineteenth centuries. According to Condorcet (1743–1794), for example, in his *Esquisse d'un
Tableau Historique des Progrès de l'Esprit Humain*
(1795), the division of philosophy into sects was
a necessary but temporary stage in the course of
philosophical thinking. From this temporary condition philosophy has freed itself step by step,

gradually replacing mere opinions by more and more rigorously tested truths.

Greece occupies a special place in this historical perspective, for her great thinkers were the initiators whose genius opened all the roads to truth. And Greek philosophy no longer suffers disparagement as a decadence, but is here recognized as instituting a real beginning. A frame is established by Condorcet in which a purely occidental philosophy represents the beginning of a historical development of philosophy. Socrates is singled out as the thinker who, rather than composing a new system, taught his successors how to use their reason; and it is the philosophy resulting from this procedure which comes to life again in Descartes, "the father of modern philosophy" (as the French still like to call him), after the long eclipse of the Middle Ages. Specifically Christian and Oriental philosophies are in this wise excluded, following Condorcet, from the immediately succeeding histories of philosophy.

In this severely restricted sense, the thinkers of the last years of the eighteenth century sought to introduce unity and continuity into the history of philosophy, while their successors in the early nineteenth century undertook actually to carry on with this program.

Up to this time, what was lacking, it was generally now agreed, was a full blown sense of the historical. In an article published in 1791, for example, Reinhold, the above-mentioned critic of eclecticism, pleaded, like Condorcet, for a history of philosophy which should present the thought of the past, not negatively, as a history of the follies of men, but positively, as their wisdom, not unfairly judging them in terms of later ideas, but rather in terms of their own professed aims and actual accomplishments.

And according to Tennemann, in his *Geschichte der Philosophie,*[8] the history of philosophy ought not to presuppose any idea of philosophy, but instead ought to present the gradual formation of philosophy, of the efforts of reason to realize the idea of a science of the laws of nature and of liberty.

However, Erdmann charges both Tennemann and his French contemporary, De Gerando[9] with interposing their own views of philosophy in their accounts of the views of their predecessors. Tennemann, for example, judges even the earliest systems from his own Kantian standpoint. Nevertheless, De Gerando is reputed to be "the first writer who regards the history of philosophy from a philosophical point of view," by none other than the great historian, Erdmann himself.[10]

What indeed justifies this ascription of a "philosophical point of view" to these historians, is precisely the fact that in theory at least, if not in practice, they recognized the validity of the demand that the historian should adopt some definite and explicit principles of interpretation and evaluation of the systems of the past, some unifying bond linking those systems with each other in an intelligible fashion, rather than presenting them as so many entirely unrelated and arbitrary intellectual constructions.

The leading authorities in this field in the early nineteenth century met this demand in two different ways.

De Gerando (1804), for example, adopted a method, for which he acknowledged his indebtedness to Bacon, of an inductive and comparative sort. By means of this method, he first ascertained the basic questions (assumed to be few in number) to which each system presumed to find the answers. Then, by examining these answers, in turn, De Gerando found that he could arrange the systems themselves in natural classes. When reduced to this kind of order, finally, the systems could be compared with each other, and, considering each one as an experiment carried out in the interests of the march of the human spirit, the historian could judge which were the best.

The principle of unity underlying this procedure was psychological; that is to say, the classification of the different doctrines was based upon elementary psychological factors allegedly inherent in the human mind.

As a matter of fact, and judging by its results, Victor Cousin's method was not very different. In both cases the method might be described as a sort of a cross or combination of the classificatory procedures of the science of botany and a purely speculative psychology.

Obviously this is in effect to reduce the history of philosophy to psychology; it is to replace the temporal succession of doctrines by their cross-sectional classification, and is to deny, even if such a denial be contrary to the author's intentions, the very idea of a history in any pregnant sense of the word.

In extenuation of this serious defect, however, it should be noted that, logically speaking, classification *is* an obvious and well-nigh universal first attempt at introducing order into a complex manifold of any sort. And only after its minor virtues and serious defects in understanding have been explicitly exposed in practice, and some more adequate method of ordering has been hit upon, can any more fruitful procedure be developed. And at a time when psychology and philosophy were still so indistinguishably entangled with each other as to preclude any possibility of realizing clearly the distinctions, which even much later thinkers have found it exceedingly difficult to grasp, between the merely psychological and the full-blown philosophical, thinkers may certainly be excused for not recognizing the defects due to failure to maintain any such distinctions. And as will presently only too obviously be apparent, certain later and much more historically sophisticated philosophers must be charged with much the same shortcomings.

But an impetus once definitely acquired, in however imperfect a fashion, is not soon or easily to be dissipated. And viewed in this light, it becomes clear that by the dawn of the nineteenth century an essential long first step has been taken, which leads along a road, encumbered with many turnings and obstacles, no doubt, but about whose general direction there can be no question—the direction, namely, of conceiving of the history of philosophy as an integral part or element of philosophy itself.

In turning in the next chapter to the second of the two ways in which, during this period, the demand for the formulation of a rationale of the history of philosophy was met, this point will become even more obvious.

2. *COMTE AND HEGEL:*
DEVELOPMENT

The second way of answering the demand for a rationale of philosophy's history is that proposed by Comte and Hegel. Each of these thinkers, in his own fashion, saw the history of philosophy as a dynamic process, in which each succeeding system figures as a necessary moment, and in which there exists a definite *liaison* between these systems.

Such an interpretation was a natural accompaniment and outgrowth of the rise of the social and moral sciences of the early nineteenth century, and was in accord, both with the Romantic movement in art and literature, and with the belief in and emphasis upon the idea of progress in all fields. It also well conforms to the way of regarding history in general as oriented, not toward a particular region or empire, but rather toward the collective civilization of the entire world—in short, toward what came to be designated as "universal history."

I

No science can be comprehended in abstraction from its history—a history inseparable from the general history of humanity, is the way Auguste Comte (1798–1857) envisaged it in his famous *Cours de philosophie positive*.[1] The present is inseparable from the past, and the present stage of intelligence is to be regarded as issuing from the preceding stages in accordance with the dynamic progress and continuity of civilization in its entirety. This continuous progress consists in the advance from the purely subjective order of the earliest times to the purely objective order marked by the positive philosophy itself.

What interests historians from this point of view, is not so much the technical portions and aspects of philosophy, as its fundamental theorems, its content as distinguished from the claims to absolute truth. Each and every system of opinions stands in relation with its epoch, and acquires its sole justification from this fact.

There is no need, for present purposes, to follow Comte in tracing out in detail the course of human thought as thus simply outlined. At the core of the theory is the famous "law of the three stages"—the theological, the metaphysical, and the positive (or scientific). Once the third definitive stage has been reached, it becomes the task of later thinkers simply to "carry on" in the spirit of positivism, toward a goal that ever recedes, while marking triumph after triumph in the supreme cause of Humanity.

Such is the grandiose vision of a thinker intellectually intoxicated, as it were, with the idea of progress. The simplicity, the excessive simplicity of this design of history, does not, of course, spell ease of execution; in fact, the "religion of Humanity" proved to be, in the sequel, but an impractical dream, incapable of realization. Yet for all that, the vision lent a powerful new impetus to historical and social studies, and forced even its detractors and critics to new efforts to trace in ever greater detail and exactness the course of human thought in all spheres.

But the course of human thought, like the course of true love, is rarely smooth. Precisely at this point in philosophy's history, a problem arises that has never since ceased to plague the authors of histories of philosophy. And indeed the problem becomes the more acute, the more original and creative is the thought of the philosopher turned historian. Although Comte himself was innocently unaware of this problem, it is implicit in his theory, as indeed it was for the theories of some of his predecessors.

Confronting all historians, and not alone philosophical ones, but in an especially virulent manner tending to infect the historian of philosophy, is the logical malady of circular reasoning. In the view of the great historian of Greek philosophy, Eduard Zeller, for example, this pernicious malady resides in the very nature of the historian's undertaking. For, on the one hand, "he alone can be said adequately to understand the history of philosophy who already possesses the true and complete philosophy"; and on the other hand, "he only arrives at true philosophy who is led to it by understanding history." Nor, he pessimistically concludes, "can the circle ever be entirely escaped."

II

Even more in the case of Hegel (1770–1831), than in that of Comte, this problem becomes pressing, because of the special emphasis he places upon the history of philosophy in his own system of thought. For Comte, the thought of the past is important only as *leading up to* his own "positive philosophy," with respect to which the past, as it were, makes way. But for Hegel, the thought of the past is, so he claims, an integral part of, has been taken up into, and absorbed by his own philosophy, without which his philosophy would not have been possible.

In fact, Hegel devotes over one hundred pages (in the English translation of his *Lectures on the History of Philosophy*)[2] to elaborate explanation of why he attaches such importance to the subject.

"The history which we have before us," he declares, "is the history of Thought finding itself . . . and it only finds itself in producing itself, . . . only exists and is actual" in this process—a process which has been going on for twenty-five hundred years. It follows that the history of philosophy "essentially becomes the science of Philosophy" itself.[3]

But just here it is necessary to distinguish. For in one respect, philosophy is no different from other human activities—for example, the natural and social sciences—which also have their histories. Each of these activities has what Hegel calls its "external history," that is, an account of its "origins, diffusion, maturity, decay, revival; a history of its teachers, promoters and opponents," and of its relations with religion and the State. But on the other hand, the histories of the several sciences, for example, differ in much more important respects from the history of philosophy. The steady onward movement of the former, consisting for the most part in "peaceful additions of new treasures to those already acquired" stands in striking contrast with the latter, which "seems merely to afford the spectacle of ever recurring changes . . . such as finally are no longer even connected by a common aim."

To the tyro in philosophy—and this term includes even those who have a smattering of its history—the task of that history is simply to record, in chronological order, the confusingly vast number of what he regards as philosophical "opinions" on a great variety of subjects. Such a history inevitably becomes either "an idle tale, or, if you will, an erudite investigation." The value ascribed to it is simply that it serves to stimulate one's own thoughts, and leads now and then to new ideas and "excellent reflections."

Even assuming that somewhere in this welter of opinions the truth is to be found, how is one to go about finding it? It stands to reason that if one philosophical theory be true, all the others must be, if in varying degrees, false. But how is one to select the one true theory? Each theory, in turn, "asserts its genuineness, each even gives different signs and tokens by which the Truth can be discovered; sober reflective thought must therefore hesitate to give its judgment."[4] And each new philosophy makes the claim that by it all previous philosophies are refuted, what is wanting in them is now supplied, and at length the right philosophy has been established. Quoting Scripture, the latest Pretender to the throne of Truth exclaims, "Let the dead bury their dead; arise and follow Me."— To which perhaps the most fitting reply is Peter's remark to Ananias: "Behold the feet of them that shall carry *thee* out at the door."

True enough, the sceptical questioner may exclaim; out of the philosopher's own mouth his subject stands revealed in its true light, and this revelation fully justifies the relegation of philosophy, and especially of the history of philosophy, to the very modest place it occupies in the modern curriculum of higher education. So true is it, indeed, that even the serious student of philosophy need bestow only perfunctory attention on its history. The careful and detailed study of Kant, for example, is only for erudite specialists in German philosophy, while as for Hegel himself, it is not necessary to study him at all, for one knows beforehand that his philosophy is only a sort of extremely cumbersome system of apologetics for the Christian religion in its Lutheran version; or, alternatively, only an apologia for the (undemocratic) German State, together with an absurd, jargon-laden metaphysics miscalled logic.

In reply to all such difficulties and sceptical objections, what actually has Hegel to offer?

Well, as stated previously, it is Hegel's thesis that the history of philosophy renders manifest in the diverse philosophical systems, as they appear in time, that there is only one philosophy at different stages of its development, and that the special principles upon which those systems are based are in fact branches or members of a single and ever self-identical totality. The last system in time is also in principle the richest in content, for it ideally embraces or embodies, as it were in concentrated essence, all the truths of all prior systems. Philosophy, like a living organism, is a growing, developing unity, and the diverse systems into which it differentiates itself in the course of that development stand to it somewhat as do the various parts, organs, and products of living and growing plant or animal.

But the unity-in-diversity of philosophy is of course much more profound, much more significant, than the mere metaphor would suggest. Thought, and especially philosophical thought, is of the nature of an eternal process, in which the end is ever being attained and ever being superseded. In Hegel's technical jargon, previous philosophies are *aufgehoben*—both preserved and surpassed by those which succeed them. And this, in principle, applies to that philosopher's own system, as to all others, past and to come. At all events diversity is a necessity, not as the philosophical ignoramus supposes, a serious defect, of philosophical speculation.

"The truth, the whole truth, and nothing but the truth"—this phrase, so trite and yet so full of meaning, accurately describes for Hegel the attainment of philosophy in the process of its historical development. And it is only in the conscious possession of this truth that man fully realizes his essential nature as rational and as free. Or, to put it in another way, only when and where freedom reigns can philosophy flourish to the utmost.

Unlike the achievements of science, in which case all that is valid in the work of past scientists is completely incorporated in the newest advances, and there is no remainder, nothing of permanent worth in those past achievements which is not included in those advances, the past achievements of philosophy are never left behind, but rather live on in the present, and in a sense gain rather than lose significance as a result of later developments. Whereas the scientist can afford largely to neglect all of the past history of his science save only the immediately preceding stage, from which he starts and upon which he builds, it is quite otherwise with philosophy. For the philosopher, the very nature of his subject and task becomes clear to him only in so far as his intimate knowledge of the entire history of philosophy makes it clear to him. To ignore the past is inevitably to repeat its errors, and to duplicate its shortcomings, and it is to retraverse the same ground that has already been won. Croce's famous dictum that all history is contemporary, is on Hegel's view, certainly valid with respect to the history of philosophy.

It is sometimes said, and even by those who are generally adjudged competent historians of philosophy themselves, that the philosophy of any age or people, is, in considerable measure, related to and influenced by the other interests and activities characteristic of that age and people—political and social institutions, scientific achievements, art and religion. And in some sense this is undoubtedly true; but in a deeper sense it is truer, so Hegel holds, to say that philosophical thinking is just the concentrated expression of the whole spirit of the time, of the *Zeitgeist*, which manifests itself, *mutatis*

dialectic

mutandis, in all these various ways. In this connection, what is meant by "the latest philosophy in time," which as was noted above, Hegel regards as substantially at once negating and affirming the truth of all past systems (rather than as simply "refuting" them, which he contends is an erroneous notion) may be, but often is not the work of any one philosopher—of a Dewey, say, or a Whitehead. Rather, perhaps the more usual situation is that only in the synthesis or consensus, as it were, of several rival or contending contemporary philosophies is the whole sum and substance of the thought of the time adequately embodied. That is to say, such rival philosophies represent sides or aspects of the whole truth, neglected or subordinated by others, but nevertheless legitimate and meaningful for all that, and all equally characteristic of the spirit of the time. Such is the case, for example, with early rationalism and empiricism in the eighteenth century; while perhaps the philosophy of Kant may be said most fully to express both, and even additional aspects of the thought of that age.

However that may be, dialectic, as everyone knows, is the name Hegel customarily gives to the whole process of thought, both in its temporal and in its logical dimensions. What may be called the logic of philosophical thought is thus dialectical; it is a process which, like all things human, has a temporal aspect, but it is not wholly temporal, and may indeed be described, says Hegel, as eternal, as transcending the sheer temporal order. Essential to this dialectical process is contradiction, though not the wilful arbitrary contradiction of the ignorant man, but rather that of the profound thinker who realizes that the full truth cannot be embodied in any single assertion or intellectual dogma. The popular saying that there are opposite sides to every question thus has for Hegel a genuine philosophical import.

III

Now it is precisely upon this conception of the dialectical development of philosophical thought that the many and manifold criticisms of Hegel's philosophy center. The celebrated formula for that development—thesis, antithesis, synthesis—has been attacked as an artificial straitjacket, imposed by its inventor on the immensely complex and variegated course of philosophical speculation—and on much else besides. Only to the most naive and superficial observation can the formula seem at all to correspond to the historical sequence, even when violence is done to the temporal series of philosophies in the name of an alleged "logical" connection between philosophical systems. In any case, the interconnections between philosophies are at once more complex and much looser than the formula allows. Etc., etc. In short, dialectic, as Hegel understands it, is a quasi-mechanical scheme, and the alleged logical necessity of the development is actually imposed upon it more or less arbitrarily.

With particular reference to the history of philosophy, furthermore, Hegel is specifically charged with the fallacy of circular reasoning which Zeller so acutely recognized as the stone of stumbling which the historian can scarcely avoid.

In the introduction to his magisterial *Histoire de la philosophie*[5] Emile Bréhier echoes the criticism first voiced by the great German historian of philosophy Wilhelm Windelband.[6]

A unity of the human spirit and the continuity of its development—such are the philosophical presuppositions imposed a priori upon the historian ere he begins his task. Supposedly immanent in the very nature of *Geist* or Mind, knowledge of this a priori is not justifiable by any methods available to history as such.

Hegel's reply to all such criticisms would be, in part, a frank acknowledgment that, as an historian of his subject, he must needs

> bring with him the Notion of the subject, in order to see it in its phenomenal aspect, and in order to expose the object faithfully to view . . .[7]

He further adds that

> only a history of philosophy . . . regarded as a system of development in Idea is entitled to the name of Science. . . . Only thus as a succession of phenomena established through reason, and having as content just what is reason and revealing it, does this history show that it is rational. . . . How should the whole of what has taken place in reason not itself be rational?[8]

In short, to repeat what he had said earlier, Hegel explicitly admits that "the history of philosophy cannot be treated . . . without the introduction of the historian's views." Hegel in effect bases his case on the assumption that his voice is the voice of Reason itself—of the "thought thinking thought" of Aristotle.

What is this but rationalism now read into the history of philosophy, instead of, as formerly with Descartes, embodied in self-evident truths?

In spite of such critical strictures, however, it cannot be denied that Hegel exerted a tremendous influence on, and stimulated new exertions by later generations of philosophers in the field of the history of philosophy. The core idea, as it might be called, of these Hegel-inspired historians, was simply that the history of philosophy is the re-thinking of the thought of the past in the light of the thought of the present. But this idea was left, implicit, and not explicitly stated, in the works of these historians —e.g., Kuno Fischer, Erdmann, Windelband, Höffding, *et al.*

The direct statement of this simplification, omitting the rigid conception of dialectic, with which it was only too deeply entangled in Hegel's own thinking, and presented instead as an essential feature of significantly novel new doctrines of the history of philosophy, was the work of two philosophers which will be examined at a later place in this study.

In the meantime, two similar but nevertheless distinct attempts to employ what is in some prime respects merely a refinement and deepening of Victor Cousin's doctrines in the uniting of the history of philosophy with philosophy itself will occupy the next succeeding chapter.

3. *RENOUVIER AND DILTHEY:*
THE CLASSIFICATION OF PHILOSOPHICAL SYSTEMS

Philosophers who themselves are doubtful of the pretensions of philosophy, who give up the metaphysical search for certainty in near or complete despair, sometimes have recourse to its history as a study which at least bears positive fruits of its own. That is, like all history, the history of philosophy can be dealt with in accordance with sound methodological procedures which historians have worked out for themselves. In this way, such philosophers seemingly can satisfy both their speculative tendencies and their demands for scientific objectivity and exactitude. A historian of philosophical doctrines can call himself a learned man, a *savant,* and he can manipulate his texts and bibliographies, in the same fashion as the natural scientist can manipulate his instruments. And indeed, apart from specialists occupied exclusively with one or another of the various branches of philosophy, the historian can point out that there is no contemporary general philosophical theory or system in which history does not play a considerable role, in one way or another.

During the whole course of the nineteenth century the reformulation of the doctrines of the past, and what, to use a very popular term, may be called their evolution, was one of the prime preoccupations of philosophers. This was especially true of the leading philosophers of France and Germany, due largely to the great influence of Comte and Hegel and their disciples; but the same tendency can be noted in varying degrees in other parts of the world. But in the last decades of that century, and in the twentieth century up to the immediate present, several new ways of interpreting the philosophy of the past have been proposed, and it is to these recent developments that it is now time to direct attention.

What might be described in a broad sense as sociological and psychological studies—*i.e.*, historical studies guided by considerations deriving from one or the other of these two flourishing "sciences" —exerted a powerful influence on certain historians of philosophy.

An early work by Etienne Gilson on *La Liberté chez Descartes et la théologie* (1913), for example, emphasized to such an extent the exterior "influences" to which Descartes was allegedly subject, that his philosophy appeared to issue primarily from external and as it were accidental sources, rather than from an immanent logical necessity inherent in Descartes' own thought. A sort of sociology and/or psychology of philosophy and philosophers was the natural outcome of this way of rendering philosophy's history, when carried to an excess. The philosopher was sometimes made to appear as a sort of focus of social forces, working upon him from with-

out, of which he became the unwitting instrument
or exemplar. And his philosophy was represented
as "nothing but" the resultant, the effect, of such
casual forces.

A standpoint of this kind naturally implied some
sort of historical relativism and a denial of the possibility of metaphysics.

I

The considerable influence of psychology, in
particular, on the history of philosophy has led to
the formation of special ways of reading that history.
Two names which stand out here are those of
Charles Renouvier (1815–1903) in France, and
Wilhelm Dilthey (1833–1911) in Germany. It is
significant that both of these philosophers deny the
possibility of metaphysics as a professed body of
ultimate truths, and instead conceive of philosophy
as presenting a *Weltanschauung*, a world-view,
basically deriving from psychological sources.

In both cases, again, the history of philosophy
becomes, not a single chronological series of thinkers
and their theories, but rather a plurality of theories
and systems, arranged and classified under two or
more general principles of classification.

Thus the neo-criticist Renouvier rejects the eclec-
ticisms, scepticisms, and sectarianisms of earlier historians, and finds the theories of Comte and Hegel,
issuing in the idea of a single outcome of the development of philosophical thought, equally untenable.
As contrasted with all such interpretations, Renouvier holds that the course of philosophical specula-

tion clearly demonstrates the thesis that the human mind is by nature and intrinsically antinomical, in the Kantian sense. And according to his reading of the history of philosophy, one dominating controversy, underlying all the superficial differences and disagreements of philosophical theories and systems, of all times and places, centers around the everlasting conflict between liberty or freedom and determinism or necessity.

Quite apparently, however, the "antinomy" resolves itself in favor of liberty, for such, Renouvier maintains, is the prerequisite of all philosophy. In the long run, philosophy can flourish only in an atmosphere of freedom.

Renouvier's detailed account of the history of philosophy is to be found in his *Esquisse d'une classification systématique des doctrines philosophiques.*[1] In the "Seventh Part" of that work, the author succinctly summarizes his opposition to Hegel, and precisely defines his own (antinomical) position.

Hegel's philosophy of the Absolute, envisaging the history of philosophy as an inevitable, impersonal evolutionary development, in accordance with a necessary law, allows no freedom of mind to the individual thinker, and denies to the philosopher the right to affirm or believe a single truth on his own personal account. And Hegel presents himself, as if at the end of time, as "the interpreter of the law," and as "the universal conciliator of all past ideas," who sits in universal judgment over the entire course of philosophical speculation. From such a point of view, "there can be no question of classification [of theories or ideas] but only of a series and the law of that series" (translation by the present writer) .

> But if, on the contrary, the history of philosophy being, as I have demonstrated [for this demonstration, see below], only a progressively affirmed, enlightened and constant irreducible opposition of the *sic* and the *non,* on questions of sovereign interest for thought, which logically demands this *sic* or this *non* in reply, the one excluding the other; if, I say, the affirmations and negations are in themselves valid, and enunciate specific truths or errors, and if the principle of contradiction is sound, then what philosophical doctrines call for is a classification. And this classification must be dichotomous, in terms of the most important and irreconcilable contraries, grouped subsequently, so far as possible, on the two sides, following the affinities which experience or reason makes out among them.

Chief among the antinomical oppositions in question, Renouvier finds those of thing and idea, infinite and finite, evolution and creation, happiness and duty, certainty and belief, and, above all, necessity and liberty.

He furthermore asserts that

> we can regard it as agreed upon by all philosophers truly capable of getting to the bottom of the matter, that all human knowledge is relative to human, *i.e.,* individual and personal minds, and depends upon the particular phenomena of those minds, and the form of psychical laws which they display, . . . and presupposes, therefore, . . . the existence of these personalities . . . without which nothing could be known . . .

In sum, the world as known and experienced is a
society of free, active, immortal persons, under the
sovereignty of the Deity. Ideas, as the only data of
conscious experience, bear the stamp of relativity,
so that human knowledge consists of a grasp of the
relations between things, and all objects are phenomenal appearances.

Such a brief *résumé* of Renouvier's way of interpreting the history of philosophy cannot, of course,
do full justice to it. But that each individual philosopher has it within his power, and in virtue of his
freedom of mind will exercise that power, to adopt
whichever of two possible opposed positions on any
basic question or problem makes the strongest appeal
to him as a personality, may be said to be the central theme of Renouvier's doctrine. As he sees it,

> the affirmation of a moral order in the world, or of
> a non-moral order, the acceptance of the postulates
> of practical reason, or a preference of the Thing, are
> for the thinker, acts of his personality, no less than
> systematic combinations of ideas. The history of phi-
> losophy and its traditions, in the absence of personal
> conviction, can exercise no influence on the thinker's
> choice.

No philosopher can surrender his personal respon-
sibility on this absolutely basic point.[2]

Neither can an enumeration of the "influences,"
social, educational, and so forth, making up the
"spirit of the age," with all its special interests, problems, and the like, do more than account for variations on the main drift of a personal line of thought.

It will naturally occur at once to anyone confronted with Renouvier's views that out of his own mouth he stands convicted of a vast over-simplification of the actual diversity of philosophical theories throughout the ages. That immense diversity, it will be urged, cannot possibly be reduced to simple contradictory opposition, to say nothing of the implicit reduction of the intellectual personalities of philosophers to just two fundamental types.

Even granting for the moment that Renouvier's list of basic antinomies is fairly exhaustive—and this is a large concession—it still leaves entirely out of account the multifarious combinations and interminglings, the crossfertilizations and hybrid products —to use a convenient biological metaphor—that actually arise in the course of speculation. It is even less instructive, one might reasonably contend, to reduce the rich diversity of philosophical theories to just two basic types, than it would be to effect the same reduction in the realm of biological phenomena. And in the latter sphere even the division into flora and fauna becomes blurred to the vanishing point under close scrutiny.

And this is to disregard, for the time being, the whole question of the logic of classification, considered, not as a matter of mere convenience for certain practical purposes, but as opening the way to a real understanding of fundamental philosophical issues. On this very important point more will be said at the conclusion of the present chapter.

Here it only remains to observe that Renouvier's basic purpose in this way of reading the history of philosophy is to establish a firm foundation for his own personal philosophy—the very same charge which he levels against Hegel.

Later French philosophers, recognizing the lack of objectivity in this procedure, deliberately sought to overcome the defect, as they regarded it. Hamelin and Boutroux, for example, strive to present the history of philosophy as an integral part of philosophy itself, rather than as merely foreshadowing their own theories or those of any of their contemporaries. This, for example, is the spirit animating the great historical work of Emile Bréhier previously cited in the present study. As he sees it, the history of philosophy reveals neither a simple law or formula of development, nor a progression toward some single goal, some one definitive philosophical doctrine. Rather, it teaches the lesson that philosophical thought is constantly being subjected to renewed questioning, constantly in danger of degenerating into lifeless formulae which betray its spiritual significance. "The life of the spirit," Bréhier concludes, is in the work, and not in a presumed truth acquired once and for all."[3]

But while such a declaration may serve admirably, as it certainly does in Bréhier's own case, as a hueristic principle to guide the historian, it can hardly be said to be more than a restatement of the problem facing the philosopher rather than a solution to it.

II

At a more appropriate point in this study other ways of construing the history of philosophy by

French thinkers will be examined. In the meantime, another psychologically oriented version somewhat resembling that of Renouvier, but rather
more elaborate, calls for attention.

This version is the work of the German thinker
Wilhelm Dilthey (1833–1911). Best known for his
special interest in the "mental (or humanistic)
sciences" (Geisteswissenschaften), and especially in
history, he is commonly regarded as one of the
leaders in the study of the logic and epistemology
of all such sciences, which he distinguishes sharply
both as to object and method, from the natural
sciences.

The material upon which the following exposition of Dilthey's interpretation of the history of
philosophy is based, consists (a) of a translation, by
Kluback and Weinbaum, of an excerpt from Dilthey's Gesammelte Schriften,[4] entitled "The Types
of World Views and Their Unfoldment within the
Metaphysical Systems";[5] (b) an essay, "The Essence
of Philosophy" (included in Vol. V of the G. S.)
translated by S. A. Emery and W. T. Emery;[6] and
(c) two works by H. A. Hodges, Wilhelm Dilthey:
An Introduction,[7] and The Philosophy of Wilhelm
Dilthey.[8]

Dilthey's intellectual make-up may be provision-
ally described as a unique blend of Comtean Positivism and neoKantianism. While voicing great respect for Hegel, in Dilthey's estimation Hegel, like
too many other philosophers, has a mistaken con-
fidence in metaphysics as affording the means for
a solution to the "riddles" of life and the world.
Metaphysical systems come and go, while their very

diversity proves that their competing claims are without foundation.

But this scepticism with respect to the validity of any one metaphysical system is by no means the whole story, and those critics who describe Dilthey as a sceptic do so only at the expense of ignoring essential features of his philosophy. Despite its repeated failures, Dilthey holds, there is something of importance to be learned from the repeated efforts of metaphysics to attain its goals, and it is precisely to the history of philosophy that one must turn in order to discover what that something is.

Or rather, it is to that history when comprehended and interpreted in the light of what Dilthey considers to be the fundamental facts about the constitution and workings of the human mind, which will reveal the true significance of metaphysics, as well as of much else besides.

One such fact, for instance, apparent to the analytical and descriptive psychology of which Dilthey professes to be the author, is what he calls "lived experience" (*Erlebniss*)—the experience of the conscious living human being in contact and relation with its natural, social, cultural and historical environment. As the translators of *The Essence of Philosophy* explain, in their Preface, "*Erlebniss*" means

> any cognitive, affective, or conative act or attitude which is conscious, but distinguished from the object to which it is directed, and not itself the object of any other act or attitude. We do not know, feel and will them; we know, will and feel *through* them.

In short, conscious human life is according to Dilthey a structured, dynamic, ongoing organization, and its functioning is in terms, turn and turn about, of one or the other of these three basic attitudes. Each of these attitudes has its characteristic goals or aims, for all human activity is teleological in nature. And the highest goals, by hallowed tradition designated as beauty, goodness and truth, are reached in the attainments of art, religion and philosophy. Freedom is both the prerequisite and the condition of minds devoted to their highest aim and accomplishments in these spheres of activity. For the aims are perfectly universal in nature, not tied down and restricted to, or bounded by specific theoretical or narrowly practical considerations. Rather, they answer to the inmost requirements or demands by and through which mankind realizes its own ultimate destiny, and they and they alone give the final meaning to human life.

But men differ, one from the other, as everyone is well aware; they have, as the current expression goes, different "personalities" or "characters," formed by a multitude of circumstances in which they live out their lives. Different ages, different cultures, different experiences in the course of their lives, all play their parts in forming these personalities, and consequently in determining their works of art, their religions, and their philosophies.

Great as this diversity is however, the historian (and only the historian) has resources to master it, and the means whereby to reduce it to order. For one thing, by an inductive and comparative empirical investigation[9] he discovers that, at least implicitly in art and religion and explicitly in metaphysical systems, throughout the ages, the leading artistic, devout and speculative productions respectively issue in, or give expression to what Dilthey calls World-views *(Weltanschauungen)*.

Designed to solve the ultimate "riddle of life and the world," and hence to give substantial meaning to human existence as *all* such world-views are, metaphysical systems, constituting *one* of the three great species of world-views, find their solutions in theories for which they claim absolute and universal validity—Truth. Such systems are specific products of the cognitive attitude, cognate with similar products of the conative and affective attitudes of religion and art (poetry in particular) respectively.

But, as has just been said, it is in the sphere of philosophy that World-views come to their clearest expression, and in order to show how and why this is so, Dilthey employs his interpretation of the history of philosophy as expounded in his essay *The Essence of Philosophy*.

In view of the bewildering succession of systems, theories, and problems that parade under the banner of philosophy, under constantly changing historical conditions, it seems at first that, empirically speaking, there is actually no such thing as philosophy, but only philosophies. Individual philosophers, one by one, define their subject according to their own conceptions and interests, without much regard for the original meaning of the word. Such being the case, how is one to attain the "inner unity," if indeed such there be, which can be said to "embrace the whole philosophical field?" Assuming that it could be found, this unity, this "essence" of philosophy, "would express the formative law, operative in the origin of each philosophical system, and the genetic relations, between the particular facts, falling under the law, would result from it."

Only the "historical facts" themselves serve as the raw material for the search for unity; so much is surely obvious. But by what method are these facts to be reduced to order? For that matter, this is the all-important question confronting the historian, not only of philosophy, but of all the humane studies (*Geisteswissenschaften*).

Dilthey is as aware as Zeller was, of the complexity of the problem, and especially of the danger of falling into a vicious circle. How can one gather, from the historical facts supposedly forming the field of philosophy, the essential concept of what philosophy is, without prior knowledge of the subject?

The question of method would be answered immediately if only the concept could be deduced from more general ones. This, indeed, so Dilthey charges, has been "the opinion of . . . philosophers of the German speculative school." Yet individual members of that school have been able to agree neither on a universally valid deduction, nor on universal recognition of an intuition.

As Dilthey sees it, there is only one other possibility, which he hereupon proceeds to formulate. Basing himself on his psychological findings, on what he held were the "facts" of consciousness, "lived experience," and proceeding by means of an analytical-comparative historical investigation, Dilthey worked out his interpretation of the history of philosophy. As contrasted with the rationalistic, a priori "deductions" of the Hegelians—for so Dilthey regarded them—he conceived of his method as strictly empirical.

Psychologically, it is of course the cognitive attitude which is pre-eminent in philosophy. But one must not overlook the fact that it is the whole man who philosophizes, the very same man who creates works of art, generates religious beliefs and practices, and so forth, through the whole gamut of human activities and productions.

But while great artists (poets), founders of religion, and philosophers differ in their personalities as do other men, and are equally subject to temporal and cultural conditions or "influences," a comparative study of their works yields a most important result.

This result is nothing less than the discovery of those "formative laws" of World-views whose significance for the history of philosophy was indicated earlier. These laws are to the effect that all human attitudes, including the cognitive, arise and develop as a result of the "great experiences" of life—attitudes which become firmer as the experiences repeat themselves and coalesce, and which are in accordance with the personalities or characters of the individuals involved. Thus there is not, more precisely speaking, just one attitude, characteristic of all metaphysicians, and designated as cognitive, but rather all sorts of variants of that attitude expressive of their total individual personalities. (Readers will note the resemblance, in this doctrine, to Fichte's well-known thesis that what kind of a philosophy a man has depends upon the kind of man he is; though Dilthey himself does not draw this comparison.)

This psychological doctrine finds its complement in the metaphysical systems expressive of the world-views of philosophers. Such systems have a complex "structure," answering to the demands of our human nature to know the "real world" (the cosmos), and to conceive and realize "life's ideals, its highest good, and its supreme principles of conduct."[10] "This structure is determined by an inherent psychical order according to which the concept of reality . . . is the basis for the evaluation of situations and objects . . . and, in turn, for the determination of the will." And "these three phases of consciousness," expressive of "immutable laws," finally issue in "a comprehensive plan of life, a highest good, the highest norms of action, an ideal of shaping one's personal life as well as that of society."[11]

Such a metaphysical world-view is therefore not merely an intellectual theory, but also a powerful creative force, a "practical energy," immensely effective in the solution of the most profound and comprehensive personal and social problems.

But just here the philosopher finds himself confronted with the historical fact of the vast multiplicity of world-views evolved in the course of time, by various thinkers of various races, with all the resultant diversity as yet unmastered. The natural outcome, so far as metaphysics is concerned, is a thoroughgoing relativism, or a scepticism to which there seems to be no answer. Philosophy seemingly ends in bafflement, in an intellectual *impasse*.

Dilthey, however, after repeatedly calling attention to this state of affairs, and even emphasizing it, confidently undertakes the task of mastering this vast complexity.

First of all, in its natural search for stability amidst this evolutionary conflict, the human mind, as a first result, inevitably eliminates what turn out to be the shallower, less useful of these world-views, and conserves those "which promote a deeper understanding of life and lead on to more useful goals of life."[12]

This selective process, in the course of time, leads to an increasing perfection of the structures of the survivors, just as in biological phenomena. An "inner dialectic," as Dilthey likes to call the process of the formulation of ever more perfect, more complex and comprehensive structures, guides the work of the great philosophers; not dialectic in the formalized Hegelian sense, but rather a dialectic conceived of as the actual historical order of ideas, generated in human minds immersed in successive cultures, and occupied with ever new problems of universal scope and significance.

Now when these structures, these metaphysical systems, which are, as it were, fittest to survive, are subjected to a "comparative historical method," certain important findings appear. Just "as the comparative study of languages, religions, and states reveals certain types, developmental lines and regularities of change, so we can demonstrate a typology of world-views."[13]

Common to all such world-views, and a permanent feature of their evolutionary development, is the endeavor "to lift life to full awareness of cognition of reality, of appraisal of life, and of active performance through our wills." But in spite of a persistent "will to stability," to "fixity," manifested in this endeavor, "mankind has not made the slightest progress," in over two thousand years in attaining the goal of universal validity. Instead, certain great types of World-views endlessly compete with each other, and though "individual phases" and subordinate structures within one type or the other may be rejected or refuted, the main types persist through all time, for "they have their roots in human life" itself, and are a "law unto themselves," at once both essentially "undemonstrable and indestructible."

How many are there of these types, and how are they distinguished from each other?

Dilthey finds that there are just three persistent types of philosophical World-views, which he names, respectively Naturalism, the Idealism of Freedom, and Objective Idealism (not to be confused with the Hegelian meaning of this phrase).[14] These types have their psychological source in the attitudes and personalities of their authors, in accordance with Dilthey's thesis outlined above. Metaphysicians, for example, stamp "the particular constitution of their own lives on systems of conceptions which claim universal validity. The typical element therein is identical with their character, and is expressed in their particular order of life."[15] In this sense, each World-view is "intuitive," that is, originates from its author's "immersion in life." Hence, properly to comprehend a metaphysical system, the student needs a "sympathetic and deep penetration" beginning from his own life-experience, into the life-experience of its author.

But in order to discover that there are three principal types of World-view, rather than some other number, the student must also avail himself of the comparative historical method. Only by constant practice, by testing its results again and again, can this combined psychological and historical procedure avoid the errors of hasty generalization, and the abstract labelling of philosophical theories, which is far too common a vice of historians of philosophy. Indeed, Dilthey even goes so far at one point, in emphasizing the provisional nature of the results obtained by his procedure, as to declare that

> I would leave it to individual choice of a systematizer whether he makes logical arrangements other than mine, as, *e.g.*, by coupling both forms of Idealism, or by joining Objective Idealism and Naturalism. . . . The whole purpose of this definitional separation of types is to enable us to look more deeply into history from the vantage point of life itself.[16]

And, on occasion, he remarks that the distinctions marking off the types from each other sometimes become blurred and that there is much giving and taking between them.

No doubt some critics will see in such qualifications a serious defect in the whole procedure. More sympathetic critics, on the other hand, might point out that Dilthey is only frankly calling attention to the limitations and defects inherent, from a

strict logical point of view, in any system of classification of a complex subject-matter. And they might
add, in further extenuation, that it is part of the
very strength and spirit of the empiricism which
animates to so large a degree Dilthey's thinking, to
be thus clearly aware of the provisional, tentative
nature of its findings.

Leaving the matter there, at least for the moment,
it is now appropriate to set down the lists of phi-
losphers whom Dilthey assigns to each of his three
allegedly persistent types of philosophical speculation, together with the general differentiae of the
types themselves. Dilthey's *The Philosophy of Existence* and Hodge's *The Philosophy of Wilhelm Dilthey* will serve as convenient guides in this undertaking.

1. *Naturalism*. According to this line of thought,
"man is determined by nature." The structure of
this system is the same from Democritus to Hobbes
and beyond, sensationalism forming the basis of
its theory of knowledge, materialism its metaphysics,
capped by a "double-sided practical attitude," made
up of (a) the will to pleasure, and (b) "reconcili-
ation with the overwhelming and utterly strange
course of life, by contemplative subjection under this
course." Democritus, Protagoras, Epicurus, in ancient times, Hobbes, the encyclopedists, later ma-
terialists (and, as a further development under the
influence of the critical consciousness, recognizing
the phenomenal character of the physical world),
Hume, Comte, Mill and Spencer,—and so on down
to contemporary representatives—are the advocates
of this World-view.

Naturalism, however, is constrained by a "restless dialectic" to formulate "ever new conceptions of man's position in world and life." In fact, it is caught in a vicious circle; it starts from the phenomenon of consciousness, and yet tries to derive what only exists in consciousness—e.g., sensation and thought—from motion. Thus the "correlation" of the physical and the spiritual meets with "strong doubts," while naturalistic ethics "reveals its insufficiency for making the evolution of society comprehensible."

2. *The Idealism of Freedom.* Representatives of this line of thought are bound together by especially close bonds of fellow-feeling, by violent antagonism toward all versions of Naturalism, and by a less violent opposition to pantheism and Objective Idealism. Based on the inner experience of free will, the Idealism of Freedom exalts personality, interprets the world in terms of personality, and conceives of human society as ideally a revision of all free men under self-imposed moral laws, and under an absolutely free personal agent, God.[17]

Anaxagoras, Socrates, Plato, Aristotle, Cicero, the Church Fathers, Kant, Fichte, Maine de Biran, Bergson and the Pragmatists, are cited by Dilthey as exponents of this type of philosophy.

"As the metaphysical consciousness of the heroic man" (cf. Schiller, Carlyle), this World-view is indestructible and will come to life in every great man." But there is nevertheless a serious flaw implicit in it, in that "it is unable to define and scientifically demonstrate its principle in a universally valid manner." Opaque to the logical understanding

are such fundamental concepts as substance, caus-
ality and Deity, and the relations between fact and
value. And here again "a dialectic begins to work,
which restlessly advances from one possibility to
the other, without ever being able to solve its
problem."

3. *The Objective Idealism.* Under this heading
are embraced "the central mass of philosophical
systems," and the "bulk of all metaphysics," and like
the other types of World-views, Objective Idealism
has its advocates in all periods of philosophy. Central
to it, is "the contemplative attitude" in which "our
sensual life . . . is expanded into a kind of universal
sympathy." Reality becomes animated with the
supreme values of goodness, beauty and truth. On
this view, the universe is an organic, concrete, individual whole, whose parts are also individuals.
The organic relation of whole and parts, in this
sense, replaces the logical relation, as commonly
understood, of universal to particular. Epistemolog-
ically, intellectual intuition plays an important role
in this third type of World-view.

Representative thinkers are Heracleitus, Parmenides, the Stoics, Giordano Bruno, Spinoza, Leibniz,
Hegel and Schleiermacher, Renouvier [?], Green,
and Bradley.

However, metaphysics of this type can "express
only symbolically what is contained in the formula
set up by Objective Idealism for understanding the
interrelation of the world. It can . . . never be
grasped by cognition." Once again "a restless dialectic . . . drives one on from one system to another,

until all possibilities are exhausted and man recognizes that the problem can never be solved."

In *The Essence of Philosophy,* its author sums up the results of his psychological and comparative historical findings as follows: "In one sense the result . . . is negative. . . . The great oppositions of standpoints, contending with equal force, . . . assert themselves over against one another with equal justification."[18] As for combinations of selected portions of these basic types, or attempted syntheses of them in one all-embracing system, *à la* Hegel, the result can only be failure, since the relation between the types, is not, as Renouvier mistakenly held, logically antinomical, and their inexpungable differences are rooted in life itself.

Is there then only an eternal conflict of rival philosophies, with no prospect of resolution—a state of affairs which spells nothing but scepticism in metaphysics and an unrelieved relativism so far as the history of philosophy is concerned?

Not at all. In Dilthey's view, it is true, it does mean a gradual dissolution of the power of metaphysical speculation, as thinkers gradually come to realize the impossibility of attaining a definitive system of universally valid knowledge. But when thus eventually divested of the incubus of metaphysical speculation, philosophy will show itself to consist of a group of diverse functions—especially logic and epistemology—which will clarify and systematize the methods of the sciences and the presuppositions, goals, and limits of scientific knowledge. In addition, there are other such legitimate branches of philosophy as ethics, philosophy of law, of religion, of art, etc. In all these guises "philosophy appears as only the most consistent, vigorous, and comprehensive thinking . . . separated from the empirical consciousness by no fixed boundary."[19]

And over and above these diverse services rendered by philosophy, there is also one standpoint above all three persisting but irreconcilable types of World-views, namely the standpoint of what Dilthey calls "the historical consciousness" itself.

By the very procedure which he has followed, the historian of philosophy has in effect raised "the human mind above the conviction rooted in its finitude, that in one of these World-views it has grasped the truth itself." The historian's objectivity enables him "to assume a standpoint above them all. In him the historical aspect of consciousness is perfected."[20]

Descriptive history assumes the task of conceptual mastery of types of World-views, and what that history teaches is a grasp of the relationship between life and metaphysics; that is, between the three basic types of philosophical personalities and the three types of metaphysical theories—subject as they are to the inner "restless dialectic" of a quasi-evolutionary development.

"Beyond that," Dilthey confesses, "I dare not go. We lack the knowledge of the formative law according to which life shades over into, and becomes differentiated into certain metaphysical systems."[21] But that life does thus "shade over" and "differentiate" itself in the manner described, Dil-

they is convinced. Thus "the last word" of the mind
which has once risen to this comprehension

> is not the relativity of World-views, but the sovereignty
> of mind in relation to each single one of them, and
> also the positive consciousness of how, in the different
> forms of mental attitudes the one reality of the world
> exists for us.[22]

In another passage, Dilthey declares that these
World-views

> are grounded in the nature of the universe and the
> relation of the finite knowing mind to it. So each of
> them expresses one side of the universe within the
> limits of our thought. Each is herein true. But each
> is one-sided. It is not granted to us to see these sides
> all at once. The pure light of truth can be seen by
> us only in variously broken rays.[23]

Is this, and other such statements, an expression
of becoming philosophical modesty, of scepticism,
of historical relativism, of psychologism, or of yet
some other sort, more complex and not precisely
reducible to any such description, but a kind of
mixture of them all? To put it paradoxically, "the
sovereignty of the mind" as manifested in "the
historical consciousness," which reveals "the finitude
of every historical phenomenon, . . . the relativity
of every sort of belief," spells "the liberation of
man."

> With it, man attains the sovereign power to wring
> from every experience its content, to surrender wholly

> to it. . . . As if there were no system of philosophy
> and no faith which could bind man. Life becomes
> free from knowledge by concepts; mind becomes sov-
> ereign in face of all thought. . . . And in contrast
> with the relativity, the continuity of the creative force
> makes itself felt as the central historical fact.[24]

Such pronouncements, unfortunately, tend to mystify the reader rather than to clarify Dilthey's position. One meaning possibly to be extracted from them is to the effect that philosophy is no substitute for life, for actual "lived experience" —to make use of Dilthey's phrase. And if this interpretation be permitted, then no one surely will venture to oppose it. As Dilthey himself has made fairly plain in other contexts, the task of philosophy is, rather, to think as coherently and comprehensively as possible, in order to render an intelligible account of human experience, and not at all to proffer a surrogate for that experience.

At all events one point is clear. Namely, that it is to the "historical consciousness" that Dilthey looks above all for insight and understanding. It functions in his thinking, one may say, in the light of the preceding exposition, as a sort of meta-physical ultimate. And for this reason the common charge levelled against Dilthey, of advocating a kind of "historicism," certainly seems justified.

On the other hand, the tentative, unfinished character which all commentators are agreed attaches to Dilthey's writings, makes it unprofitable to carry very far critical examination of historicism as such, especially since a more fully explicitly developed version of it awaits attention in the next chapter of this study.

III

What does call for a little further consideration here is the doctrine, shared in common by Renouvier and Dilthey, and already adumbrated by certain earlier thinkers,[25] that the history of philosophy reveals the existence of not just one, but of some higher number of distinct, more or less parallel lines of thought persisting throughout its course. This contention, now more clearly stated, is certainly important enough to demand examination on its own account, quite apart from its entanglements with other issues in the philosophies of these two thinkers.

A considerable amount of evidence from history itself lends support to the idea. In actual practice, many historians of philosophy group thinkers of one period or another into schools, with no thought of doing violence to the doctrines of individual philosophers in the process. Plato and Platonists, Aristotle and Aristotelians, Stoics, Epicureans, etc., etc., in the West, and a corresponding number of different schools in the Orient, are familiar examples, about which no question is ever raised as to the appropriateness of the classification. There may be, and sometimes is, controversy about assigning a given thinker to one school rather than to another, and there are occasional instances of thinkers who defy classification; but such exceptions do not deter historians from setting up the classifications, which on the contrary they seem to regard as an obviously legitimate and illuminating procedure.

Certainly also there are specific persisting lines of thought characteristic of various branches of philosophy, e.g., logic and ethics. In the former, there have always been and doubtlessly always will be recurrences of "formal" logic, and just as frequently, their opponents. Similarly in ethics, there have always been and will continue to be hedonists and the inevitable opponents of hedonism. And so forth and so on, even to metaphysicians and anti-metaphysicians.

Does not this state of affairs, this apparently ineradicable and characteristic trait of philosophy in its historical dimension, serve to suggest that such thinkers as Renouvier and Dilthey are, in some sense, at least partly in the right, in general terms, if not in specific detail, so far as the issue of classification is concerned?

Renouvier's thesis that human thought is intrinsically antinomical, and Dilthey's thesis that three types of World-views derive from the three basic mental attitudes toward life and the world, are, of course, variants of psychological theories upon whose validity the respective philosophical theses stand or fall. When confronted with each other, however, and whatever superficial plausibility those psychological theories may appear to have—or rather, those supposedly incontestable psychological facts, as these two thinkers would each call them—they lose all claim to such a status. At least one of the two, must be wrong, and quite probably both may be!

Moreover Dilthey, for his part, frequently calls attention to the tentative character of his threefold classification; another philosopher, he admits, might, with as much justification, prefer a two-fold or a four-fold scheme. In other words, as was mentioned in a previous context, a mere classification is logically a weak device, useful only to the extent that it affords some help in dealing, on an empirical level, with recalcitrant material that temporarily at least resists a more systematic, more theoretically profound treatment.

Such as it is, moreover, it is an elementary logical principle that a classification, for other than frivolous purposes, should be based on as many and as significant features of the material to be classified as possible, rather than on extraneous considerations of any sort. But the psychological make-up of groups of thinkers or of individual philosophers is just such an extraneous factor, when it is, or should be, a question, rather, solely of the make-up, of the content, of the philosophical theories themselves.

Rejecting, accordingly, as irrelevant to philosophical purposes, the psychological doctrines of Renouvier and Dilthey, respectively, do their classifications otherwise conform to the above-mentioned criteria? So complex is the material—nothing less than the entire history of philosophy—that it seems a priori incredible that it could all be adequately ordered under so few as two or three heads, in such a way as to do even elementary justice to the vast diversity of theories and systems which must be included.

And this is not all. For an even more serious difficulty is inherent in the very special nature of the material to be classified, to say nothing of its immense complexity. Dilthey indeed recognizes this difficulty, the recognition taking the form of his claim that as a representative of "the historical consciousness" he stands above the conflict of the three basic types of contending metaphysical systems. It is precisely from this supposedly superior vantage point, that he finds it logically possible to condemn them all in respect to their respective pretensions to "universal validity." Yet surely the very same pretension inherently attaches to his own position. In his assertion that metaphysical systems eternally checkmate each other on this vital point, he proclaims the truth as he sees it; that is to say, his own assertion must be universally valid, or it is nothing.

Again, it is as an inference from the classification which Dilthey has drawn up, and not as an essential feature of that classification, that his assertion functions in his thought. As it stands, the classification reveals only that there are three distinct species of philosophical systems, set off from each other by a complex of differentiae, each species being carried forward by an "inner dialectic." Thence it appears that the classification poses a problem, insoluble so far as the classification itself is concerned, which can only be solved by transcending the limits of the systems embraced by it. Only then, when he has, as he maintains himself, actually transcended those limits, can Dilthey take the final step of presenting his solution. But obviously, in such circumstances, another historian, who might even go as far as to concur in Dilthey's classification, might still draw inferences as to its import, quite divergent from those drawn by Dilthey from the same material. For instance, such a historian, noting Dilthey's observation that one species of philosophical systems contains the "central mass" of those systems, and "the bulk of metaphysics," might infer from this state of affairs that the other two species thus revealed themselves as unstable deviations from the norm, and hence as not belonging to the main line of philosophical speculation. And so forth and so on.

Actually, of course, and as Renouvier for his part seems clearly to recognize, no philosopher can profess to "stand above" the conflict of philosophical theories and view them, as it were from the outside, from a position of privilege. Whatever his position or theory may be, it inevitably claims assent or arouses opposition, on allegedly philosophical grounds, quite as do all other theories. In this respect, at least, though not necessarily with the specific significance which Renouvier attaches to it, Renouvier stands on firmer ground.

As a final comment, no one can fail to be struck by the emphasis, common to the two thinkers, placed upon the "personalities" of the philosophers in the formulation of their theories. And that something must indeed be accorded to the personality of the philosopher in this respect is, or should be, generally recognized. One thing which distinguishes philosophy from science is, precisely, the "impersonality" that is an essential mark of the latter, as contrasted with the stamp of his personality which shows through even a great philosopher's most abstruse speculations. And what observation is more frequently made about philosophy, than that "there is something personal about it," though what and how much significance should be accorded to this feature is a question that is rarely broached?

Although they cannot be credited with the discovery of this characteristic of philosophy, Renouvier and Dilthey do manifest the tendency of discoverers to overemphasize the importance of their discoveries. If, indeed, the personality-factor of philosophy, as it may be called, were as important as these two thinkers make it out to be, then the last judgment to be pronounced on the whole philosophical enterprise, not excluding the theories of these thinkers themselves, would be that of its inevitable subjectivity and illogicality. In the last analysis, the history of philosophy, for both Renouvier and Dilthey, takes its place as a chapter, though admittedly a long and exceedingly complex one, in the psychological study of the vagaries of human nature—only that and nothing more. Or, to put the same point in another way, such a study would be the main part of philosophy itself. And this, for anyone who has eyes to see, is radically self-defeating, in that it in principle applies as exactly to the respective doctrines of Renouvier and Dilthey as to those of any other philosophers.

It is a true if trite saying that one can never judge the full import of a theory until it has somehow been tested in practice. Thus it is a great service, rendered by the two philosophers whose reading of the history of philosophy has been the subject of the present chapter of this study, to anyone seriously concerned to measure the import of that history. For they have amply demonstrated, once and for all, or so it would seem, that this import cannot be determined by means of a classification procedure functioning as the principal source of understanding. Without the assistance of extraneous psychological considerations, the classification of philosophical systems and doctrines will not serve the purposes of an interpretation of the history of philosophy, or any other substantial purpose; while with such assistance from psychology, the procedure serves only the unhistorical purpose of confirming the classifier's own philosophy.

4. CROCE AND COLLINGWOOD:
THE IDENTIFICATION OF
PHILOSOPHY WITH HISTORY

Owing in the main to the influence of Hegel, certain historians and philosophers, particularly in Germany, came in the course of time to re-examine the nature and presuppositions of history in general, with special emphasis on the question whether and in what sense if any, history is entitled to call itself a science *(Wissenschaft)*. The general conclusion reached by these thinkers was in the affirmative, but with a negative qualification to the effect that an important difference had to be noted between two groups of sciences—the natural sciences on the one hand, and the historical or nonnatural sciences on the other hand.

The natural sciences *(Naturwissenschaften)*, it was agreed by all concerned, are occupied with the search for universal laws, and are interested in the individual case only in so far as it embodies or exemplifies the universal. The other group of sciences, by whatever name they may be called (e.g., *Geisteswissenschaften*) are for their part mainly occupied with the individual in some sense or other—a sense specified in various ways by various thinkers.

For present purposes there is no need to follow the ramifications and variations which this general doctrine underwent at the hands of such philosophers as Windelband, Rickert, *et al.* What is, instead, all-important is the way this general conception of history and its presuppositions was utilized and developed along entirely new lines, for a bold new interpretation of the history of philosophy in particular.

As will become apparent in due course, this interpretation involves nothing less than the radical amalgamation of history (history in general) and philosophy; or, rather, the total submergence of philosophy as such in history as such. Readers will at once perceive that such a doctrine was already implicit, for example, in Dilthey's thinking, although that philosopher—humanitarian seemingly failed fully to realize such a development.

In a sense, too, the time itself was ripe for an interpretation of this sort; it might almost have been predicted in its actual appearance. For in any age or period of history there are certain dominant interests and activities which exert and spread their influence over all human concerns in that period. In the Middle Ages, for example, Religion occupied the very center of the stage; in the Renaissance, Art was centrally placed; and in a sense natural science has stood at or near the center for a very protracted period. But for a brief period at least, History took on a special significance for the leading thinkers of the time.

Now the importance of this matter, so far as philosphy is concerned, is that such a dominant interest is bound to make its influence strongly felt by philosophers as well as by all others. Thus in the Middle Ages, Philosophy was frequently described as "the handmaid of theology"; under the intoxicating influence of Romanticism, Schelling declared that Art was the "organon" of philosophy; and in recent times it has been held by some influential thinkers that to rehabilitate itself (as they see it) philosophy must become "scientific," in method, or in some other way, as the case may be.

Little wonder, then, that for at least a brief period, in the minds of some history-intoxicated thinkers, the only salvation for philosophy should be to immerse itself in history—not solely in its own history, but in history in general.

Students of the history of philosophy should of course take note of this sort of influence, and give it due weight in their studies; but, due as it no doubt is, to obvious psychological and sociological considerations, they must at the same time beware of confusing such an influence with a *logical* justification for a philosophical theory. But on this point more can more appropriately be said in the sequel, and it is now time to examine the actual, specific working-out of the new reading of philosophy and its history, as it developed under that influence.

I

The distinguished Italian philosopher and literary critic, Benedetto Croce (1866–1952) deserves one's first attention in this connection.

Croce greatly deepens and extends the distinction, already mentioned, between history and natural science, to the point of maintaining that the latter yields, not genuine knowledge, but rather is made up of "pseudo-concepts," serving pragmatic ends only. The universal laws of science are abstractions, and fail to disclose the nature of the individual, which alone is real.

In the light of this thesis, what is urgently called for is a new approach to history, and a re-examination of its significance for, and relation to philosophy. And with this problem Croce was seriously and continuously occupied throughout his life, as the amount of space devoted to it in his writings amply testifies.

His earliest theory of the nature of history, which largely assimilates it to art, bears the significant title *La Storia ridotta sotto il concetto generale dell'arte* (1893). But in later works, while still stressing the important enough sense in which history is an art, he no longer regards it in exactly the same light as the so-called fine arts. The main difference, as Croce comes to see it, is that, although both history and fine art are centered on the individual, history distinguishes, as art does not, between the existential real and the merely imaginary.

When it came to the writing of his *Logic*, published in 1909,[1] however, Croce was faced with the necessity of making this distinction more precise and intelligible. This task he carried out in terms of his theory of the logical judgment, and accordingly that theory calls for a brief exposition here.

Traditionally, logicians have classified (categorical) judgments as singular or individual—This A is B—, particular—Some A is B,—and universal—All A is B.

Now according to Croce, every historical statement is a perfect example of an individual existential judgment. That is to say, the subjects of which history treats are each and every one either individual to begin with, or easily reducible to such as are. This state, this general, this war, this act of statesmanship, and the like, are typical examples of subjects of historical judgments. Thus what Croce calls "the first condition" of historical knowledge is that something be *"intuited,* and thereby transformed into the subject of the individual judgment, . . . into historical narrative."[2]

But what of the predicate of such judgments?

Here is where what Croce calls "the logical element" comes in. By the logical element he means concepts. Concepts such as "crime," "nation," and, in short, all the universals serving as predicates of historical judgments presuppose a system of ethical and political philosophy. But in the language of logic, concepts are universals, and hence the individual judgment of history is universal in the sense that its predicate is a concept of which a definition can be framed. In short, the historical judgment is, actually, a "synthesis" of an individual and a universal judgment. (All definitions are universal judgments, according to Croce.)

The next point is a crucial one. It follows, so Croce maintains, from the preceding consideration, that one of the essential elements of historical narrative is philosophical in character. Or, to put the same point in a more striking way, since the prime function of philosophy is to fix the meaning of concepts, which, as actual functions of thought exist only as predicates of historical judgments, philosophy and history turn out to be inseparable from each other—to be, in effect, one and the same. Or, in what Croce considers to be other but equivalent terms, philosophy, in virtue of its traffic in concepts, may aptly be described as the methodological moment of history.

This thesis of the identity of philosophy and history is briefly asserted in Chapter Four of his *Logic,* and elaborated upon in his *Teoria e Storia della Storiografia.*[3] Nevertheless there arises at this point —if not indeed before—in the mind of the average reader of these works an uncomfortable impression of being willy-nilly impelled to the acceptance of very important, unorthodox doctrines, for which their author offers what is at best only superficially plausible support. But in spite of this serious defect in Croce's mode of presentation, and in spite of what one is tempted to call the illogicality infecting his entire *Logic,* by means of which he has effected this alleged identification of history and philosophy, he does at least succeed in calling attention to certain prima facie valid considerations which must be faced by anyone interested in the questions with which the present work is occupied.

There is the assertion, for instance, that the various branches into which history is usually divided—political, social, history of art, of religion, etc.—are mere practical conveniences, and do not reflect or stand for any intrinsic divisions of the subject; rather, history is the history of humanity in all of its aspects, and in that sense is one and entire.

Again, there is the dictum so closely associated with Croce's name, that "all history is contemporary." In the general sense in which Croce means it, the dictum may almost be regarded as a truism, and tacitly acknowledged by all historians. For what is more commonly recognized and practiced than the doctrine that every age must write history anew, in the light of the dominant interests and ideas of the age?

But this means, according to Croce, that "philosophy also changes with history, and since history spells constant change, at every moment, philosophy at every moment is new."[4]

With further specific reference to philosophy, continuous change spells "a continuous surpassing of itself."[5] This, as Croce sees it, is the only valid sense to be attributed to "the vaunted eternity" of philosophy. And its eternity, *in this sense,* is its truth—a spiritual value. It follows that the distinction between philosophy as system, and philosophy as criticism (of other philosophies) is artificial, since "negativity," as Hegel would say, is inseparable from affirmation. "Ideas are always armed with helmet and lance, and those who wish to introduce them among men must let them make war."[6]

It follows further that the search for a "definitive philosophy," so ardently pursued by certain minds, in most if not in all generations of philosophers, is to run counter to all the teachings of history, and to the consideration that "the perpetual changing of philosophy, with the world which perpetually changes, is not by any means a defect, but is the nature itself of thought and reality."[7]

This statement should not be understood, however, in spite of the temptation to do so, in an Hegelian sense. As Croce sees it, Hegel's rigid schema of thesis, antithesis, and synthesis effectively straitjackets thought, confining it to an endless iteration or repetition, without any real advance. For that schema presupposes that there is just one basic problem—the so-called metaphysical problem of the nature of Reality—whose solution is, as it were, foreordained. On the contrary, according to Croce, and when one attends to the animating spirit rather than to the dead formulas of Hegel's *system*, one sees that real progress in philosophy, as elsewhere, depends upon the realization that—to paraphrase a saying of Heracleitus—new specific problems are ever being generated out of old solutions to past problems. It is contrary to the very idea of thought as spiritual activity that the mind should ever come to rest in a metaphysical system; or that philosophy, which is merely a name for that activity, should as it were embalm itself in any sort of formula or set of formulas. Just as Beauty and Goodness are realized only in the inexhaustible productions of artists, and in the works and deeds of men, respectively, so Truth resides only in the specific individual judgments of the minds which create it; it is realized only in the positive history of human thought, and not in some mythically envisioned, transcendental, timeless realm of "Pure Being."

To the charge that is rather obviously prompted by this contention, namely that it spells historical relativism, Croce might well answer by calling attention to his thesis that thought constantly enriches and surpasses itself with the passage of time. His accounts of the history of aesthetics, and of logic, illustrate this thesis; all previous aesthetic theories, for example, being construed as successively closer approximations to his own theory. And that theory, in turn, is destined to be supplanted, in some future time, by a still more adequate one—such, at least, is the implication.

Hordes of questions crowd in upon the reader of Croce's words, and jostle each other for urgent consideration. The dogmatic tone of much of his writing, the rather cavalier fashion in which he disposes of philosophical theories with which he disagrees, and the obvious logical gaps and other defects which mar his works, all tend to arouse opposition to his theories. And even if these flaws are treated as partly merely stylistic, and psychologically excusable, at least to some degree,—such, that is, that a well-intentioned interpreter might to a considerable extent remove or correct them, there is a limit beyond which such concessions cannot be allowed.

The crucial argument in support of the equally crucial thesis, that philosophy is just the "methodological moment of history," is based upon a logical doctrine of the judgment so absurd that no other logician could be expected to accept it; and the thesis itself is *prima facie* indefensible. The total absorption of philosophy by history, as Croce envisages it involves (to be blunt) nothing more nor less than a flat contradiction in terms. And the attractive and optimistic idea of the constant enrichment of thought, with the passage of time, even though borne out in some instances, is, in the nature of the case, hardly one that can be corroborated in all instances. Very few aestheticians would agree, for example, that Croce's aesthetic theory represented such an enrichment and advance over previous theories as he claims for it.

Nevertheless Croce has impressed certain of his contemporaries and successors sufficiently to encourage them to pursue a line of thought having much in common with his own—along with some significant differences—and thus has kept alive an interest in the question with which this study is occupied. And perhaps a philosopher, like other men, may to some extent be said to be known by the enemies he keeps; that is to say, perhaps not the least of his services to philosophical speculation consists of the stimulating opposition that he arouses in the minds of his colleagues.

II

Among such thinkers, whose thinking bears both considerable resemblance along with considerable divergence, to Croce's doctrines, is the distinguished British philosopher, R. G. Collingwood (1891–1943). Not that Collingwood should be regarded as a disciple of Croce; rather, it is mainly a case of a remarkable similarity, a parallelism, in the largely independent thinking of two near-contemporaries.

The editor of Collingwood's posthumous work, *The Idea of History* (1946), Mr. T. M. Knox, makes this point convincingly in his "Introduction" to that work.

> It was their artistic and historical interests that made both of them dissatisfied with the philosophy they had been taught; they both proceeded to study Hegel for themselves and to do original work in history; and they both worked their way . . . to an identification of philosophy with history.[8]

Exactly; moreover—and this is especially significant—Collingwood's doctrines "are elaborated in more detail and argued more carefully."

In Collingwood's *Essay on Philosophical Method* (1933), however, the author had not yet established that identification. True, he does, like Hegel, insist on the "development" of philosophical concepts— e.g., "goodness"—and on the quasigenetic interconnections of the stages of that development; in short, on the dialectical and in that sense historical nature of philosophical thinking. But the philosopher still is entitled to ask "What is goodness?" and not merely the historical question of how it has been defined in the past; and in addition to writing a history of the "idea of nature," for example, he should also work out a cosmology. (In a paper presented in 1935, Mr. Knox reveals, Collingwood actually outlined such a work.)

But by the time the *Autobiography* (1939), and *The Essay on Metaphysics* (1940) came to be written, their author had decided that "philosophy as

a separate discipline is liquidated by being con-
verted into history," and argued for the purely
historical character of metaphysics in particular.[9]

What is the precise meaning, and what are the
implications in detail of this thesis?

The answers to these questions involve the doctrine of "absolute presuppositions," which accordingly calls for examination here.

A rough synonym for that phrase is "basic assumptions," with which every reasoner is familiar as part,
so to speak, of his stock in trade. But an assumption
is subject to acceptance or rejection, at the pleasure
of the parties concerned; for a variety of reasons,
assumptions may be criticized, tested, modified, rejected, etc., etc., in the course of a scientific investigation, for example, or in practically any other field
in which systematic thinking may be in progress.
And they may be of practically any degree of gener-
ality, the most general being distinguished by the
characterization "basic," or alternatively labelled
"philosophical presuppositions." Thus one may ask,
what are the philosophical presuppositions of mathematical logic, of physical science . . . of biology, of
. . . any work in history?

There are, however, some rather subtle and very
important distinctions between such basic assumptions and Collingwood's "absolute presuppositions."
For one thing, there is a science or systematic study
of these presuppositions, and metaphysics is its
proper name. For another thing, "metaphysics is
a historical science."[10] That is to say, the real "business of metaphysics is to find out what absolute
presuppositions have actually been made by various

persons at various times in doing various pieces of scientific thinking."[11] And this task of ascertaining the presuppositions of any given thinker or age is carried out by historical analysis.

For example, as Kant revealed in the section of his *Critique of Pure Reason* entitled "Analogies of Experience," the "indestructibility of substance" was "in fact" taken for granted in his age, both by common sense and by science. And "he was right in maintaining that it had not in fact been derived from . . . experience, and that it had not been based on the results of scientific experiments, but was an absolute presupposition which underlay both everyday life and science."[12] Today, on the other hand, as Whitehead, Eddington, and others have made perfectly clear, this principle is "flatly contradicted . . . on metaphysical grounds," by men who know science from the inside and who tell us that they "do not presuppose the conservation of substance but the opposite."[13] And similarly with respect to the other "Analogies."

Another point—one which indeed furnishes the clue to Collingwood's whole line of thought.

Philosophers often yield to the temptation, make the mistake, of asking themselves the seemingly natural question, which of these principles—that of the conservation of substance, or its opposite— is "really true." That is, to generalize the question, what absolute presuppositions, or what set of them, is ultimate, good for all time, never to be called in question?

Well, according to Collingwood, the entire history of philosophy is witness to the senselessness of the question, for what it surely teaches is precisely that eternal truth or falsity is not to be ascribed to such presuppositions. What the philosopher who knows the history of his subject says, is simply that such and such presuppositions underlay the thinking of such and such ages, of such and such thinkers, and this is a historical and historically ascertained fact—or better, constellation of such facts—and that is all.

A constellation of this sort is definitive of an entire civilization in all of its aspects. It is not, actually, self-consistent, but only loosely held together, and it is subject to various strains. And "the dynamics of history" underlies the process of change, whereby these strains, this "unstable equilibrium" tend to bring into being a new constellation in virtue of the working of the "dynamic logic" of history.

History is not, of course, mere change. Take, for example, that subdivision of history known as the history of philosophy, to which a special chapter is given in the *Autobiography*, as well as numerous observations elsewhere. As Collingwood points out in that work, many of his Oxford colleagues assumed that the problems of philosophy are unchanging; "they thought that Plato, Aristotle, . . . the Schoolmen, the Cartesians, *et al.*, had all asked themselves the same set of questions, and had given different answers to them."[14] Thus the question before them was, for example, "whether Aristotle or Kant was right on the points over which they differ concerning the nature of duty." The usual outcome of such an investigation would be, as might indeed be expected, that neither was right—a status naturally reserved for their own independently arrived at conceptions.

In this wise the historical question becomes in effect wholly irrelevant to the philosophical question, and the practical outcome, in one instance, was to abolish the paper devoted to the history of philosophy in the School of Philosophy, Politics and Economics at Oxford.[15]

Well and good. But if every philosophical problem changes, in the course of time, and if the business of the history of philosophy—and note that for Collingwood, this means, of philosophy itself —is to trace that change, then what is the rationale of the process, what is the "dynamic logic" involved?

Collingwood's answer to that question, unfortunately, is not as clear and firm as could be desired, but is rather such as to leave him, like Croce, open to the charge of historical relativism. Both Professor Knox, in his "Introduction" cited above, and Professor Arthur Murphy in his review of *The Idea of History*,[16] accuse him of greatly inclining in that direction.

There are, however, other passages, in various works, the implications of which tend to ward off the charge.

In the first place "the past which an historian studies is not a dead past, but a past which in some measure still is living in the present."[17] History is concerned with processes, and processes, unlike events, have no beginnings or endings, but "turn into" one another. Process P1 turns into process P2; is, as Collingwood likes to say "incapsulated" within it, still living and active there. The very possibility of history depends, in fact, upon this consideration; only in so far as the historian can rethink, in his present context, or "re-enact in his own mind" the thoughts of the actors on the stage of history, can he do his work. And as if in return for the doctrine that philosophy is completely absorbed by history, Collingwood maintains, in this connection, that history is primarily the history of thought—which is to say that it is infused with a philosophical element (cf. Croce). For all distinctively human actions can be understood only in terms of the thoughts of which the actions are as it were the outside, the embodiment.

But in the process of change which is history, is there any such thing as progress, or is it merely a case of one constellation of absolute presuppositions supplanting another to the end of time? Twentieth century historians have become very sceptical toward the idea of progress, which so aroused the enthusiasm of nineteenth century writers. But Collingwood offers a test of progress, which he regards as definitive.

The test is as follows: Take any two successive stages of history with which the historian is thoroughly familiar, so that he can claim to reconstruct them in his own mind with sympathy and insight. Then when he asks himself whether there has been any progress in the passage from the first to the second, he must explicitly bear in mind what he is *not* asking as well as what he is asking.

He is not asking, for instance, whether the second period comes nearer to the standards of his own time. For in re-enacting the periods in question, in his own mind, he has tacitly accepted them as judged by their own standards—as periods of time having their own problems, and to be judged by their success in solving those problems and no others.

Nor is he assuming, as a basis for his history, that the question arises whether the second period did certain of the same things better than they were done in the first period. "Bach was not trying to write like Beethoven and failing; Athens was not a relatively unsuccessful attempt to produce Rome; Plato was himself and not a half-developed Aristotle."[18]

Instead, what the historian *is* asking is a question which really admits of a significant answer.

> If thought in its first phase, after solving the problems of that phase, is then, through solving these, brought up against others which defeat it; and if the second solves these further problems without losing its hold on the solution of the first, so that there is gain without any corresponding loss, then there is progress. And there can be progress on no other terms.[19]

In those terms it would be easy to cite examples of progress in science; for one example, Einstein's theory of relativity, it is generally agreed, represents just such an advance over Newtonian physics. But in the more complicated area of social affairs, exemplification, though not impossible in principle, would be much more difficult in practice, and in

the case of the history of philosophy in particular
—and for present purposes this case is all important
—such advances might be claimed by some historians
but denied by others. For example, some contemporary thinkers would claim that Kant's accomp-
plishments stood in just such a relation to the
philosophies of Hume and Leibniz, while other
thinkers would surely dispute the claim. Or consider
Croce's claim that his aesthetic theory supplanted
all preceding theories on just such grounds as
Collingwood prescribes, and the many critics of
Croce who would absolutely deny the claim.

Collingwood, himself, indeed, asserts in this very
connection that "it would be idle to ask whether
any one period of history, taken as a whole, showed
progress over its predecessor;" the historian in fact
lacks the necessary ability to take any period as a
whole.[20] At all events, there is certainly no assurance that the history of philosophy resembles what
Kant called "the sure march of science," proceeding
from one triumph to another and even greater one,
presumably *ad infinitum*.

However that may be, the *test* of progress in philosophy is no other than the test in any other field
of human activity. Always and everywhere, if an
advance occurs, it is a case of one thinker, or one
generation of thinkers, fully grasping the thought
of a predecessor or predecessors, knowing just what
the earlier problems were, and how they were solved,
disentangling the truth in those solutions from the
error, and embodying that truth in their own more
comprehensive theories. Thus such a development

is always "partly constructive or positive and partly critical or negative."[21]

Let it be said, for the purposes in view, "so far so good." But one last crucial question arises at this point. Even granting that progress, as specified by Collingwood, has been achieved in one field or another—in the history of philosophy, say. Does what has just been asserted pertain also to "absolute presuppositions"? That is, is there any sense in which philosophical achievements, as just described, but evaluated now in terms of presuppositions, instead of as previously described, in terms of specific problems solved or unsolved, can be measured? Or is the last word to be simply that one "constellation" of presuppositions gradually and eventually succeeds another, as a sheer matter of fact, and that is the end of the matter?

According to Collingwood, it would seem that the answer is affirmative, but by implication from what he explicitly says, rather than by a direct reply in so many words.

What he explicitly asserts is, that as a systematic historical science or study, metaphysics is itself, like all other history, based on its own presuppositions.[22] There is no such thing, *pace* all "realists," as an absolutely factual, presuppositionless mode of thought. Nevertheless it *is* a "fact," or alternatively, it is "true," that, for example, "Kantian scientists presuppose that all events have causes."[23] In short, the historian of philosophy can discover by his method of historical analysis, the "absolute presuppositions" which the various philosophers of the past have trafficked in (presumably including also contemporary philosophers in the list) .

And since all critical or reflective thinking occurs within an historical context, it is relative in what may be characterized as a double sense.

For one thing, it is relative to the present standpoint of the historian.

> The historian (and for that matter the philosopher) is not God, looking at the world from above and outside *(pace* Dilthey!). He looks at the past from the point of view of the present;

and at other countries from the point of view of his own.

> The point of view is valid only for him . . . but for him it *is* valid. He must stand firm in it, because it is the only one accessible to him. . . . The present is our own activities; we are carrying out these activities as well as we know how;

and, from this point of view,

> there must always be a coincidence between what is, and what ought to be, the actual and the ideal. . . . The present is always perfect in the sense that it always succeeds in being what it is trying to be.[24]

There is no place, manifestly, on this view—on this astounding view!—for self-criticism within this present context, and accordingly relativity is inevitable; so, at least, it would seem.

For another thing, the presuppositions underlying

the philosophical-historical enterprise, in Collingwood's view, are just what they are, and succeed each other in a sheer temporal order, with no such inherent dialectical or logical necessity, as, for example, Hegel evisaged. All there is to animate these presuppositions is "an internal strain" (due presumably, in part, at least, to the "looseness" pervading the constellation) and a "dynamic logic" supposedly impregnating history, but never clearly described. In the example of progress in science cited above, the change, so far as presuppositions are concerned, was, it will be recalled, from "conservation of substance" to "just the opposite." But there was no suggestion that in other instances of progress the *same sort* of change in presuppositions would occur; and in any event there is no criterion, analogous to the criterion applicable to specific problems in science or elsewhere, set up to apply to presuppositions as such.

The implication from all this is, surely, that the presuppositions of one age or thinker are just what they are; and beyond that, nothing further is to be said about them. History records, but does not judge—except to regard the present as always perfect.

The reader is left at the end of his reading with a tantalizing impression that Collingwood has *all but* worked out a tenable solution to what Professor Murphy (in the review cited above) rightly calls "a central philosophical problem"—namely, the problem concerning "the historicity of a philosophy which is nevertheless not history."

III

Looked at objectively, and in general terms, there was already implicit in Dilthey's case a view explicitly shared by Croce and Collingwood, which may be called the idealization of history. That is to say, history and historical knowledge are endowed with a position of supremacy among all intellectual activities, and allotted the function of evaluating all other human activities in its own terms. Philosophy in one way or another thus ceases to be master in its own house; it surrenders its proper place either to "the historical consciousness" (Dilthey), or in order to become "the methodological moment of history" (Croce), or to metaphysics simply defined as "an historical science" (Collingwood).

It is small consolation that such idealization of history is only an instance, among others, of a strong general tendency which can be illustrated again and again from the history of philosophy, and even from contemporary thinkers. In the case of Bertrand Russell, for example, it is something called (at one stage of his career) "the scientific method" which is invoked, to replace any sort of specifically philosophical methods or procedures, and which is to provide the intellectual salvation which philosophy, unaided by science, has allegedly hitherto failed to provide. And so forth and so on.

The point is that what all such idealizers, including the Croces and the Collingwoods, overlook, is simply that the pronouncement assigning to history or to scientific method, or to whatever, the supremacy in philosophical undertakings, is itself a bit of metaphysics, not of history, or the scientific method itself, or of anything else whatsoever. And as such it cannot escape critical scrutiny by other philosophers, and in philosophy's own terms. Not the least of the great services to philosophy of the two thinkers who have presented history in general, rather than only the history of philosophy in particular, as a sort of surrogate for philosophy, is that they have so clearly if all unintentionally revealed this very important fact.

And thus the way has at last been cleared for the examination of still another highly original, one might almost say inspiring conception of philosophy and its history. Hindsight, if not foresight, sees it as almost inevitable that such an idealization of history was bound to be tried, in view of the very special prominence everywhere accorded to history in the recent past. And perhaps it is as an equally natural and almost inevitable reaction to such an excessive estimation of history, that another thinker should, in a very real sense, while paying lip-service to the Muse of history, so construe history as in effect largely—though not entirely—to negate it. That such an outcome should issue from the speculations of a representative, as he is usually regarded, of a prominent contemporary movement in philosophy, renders it only the more important and interesting.

5. *KARL JASPERS:* THE GREAT THINKERS

I

One of the best known of contemporary German philosophers, Karl Jaspers, gives a great deal of weight to the history of philosophy in his own thinking. An unwilling victim of the seemingly irresistible tendency among philosophers to classify their colleagues into schools, Jaspers is commonly referred to as an "existentialist." But while he is quick to acknowledge his special regard for, and indebtedness to Kierkegaard and Nietzsche, two of the most frequently cited sources of existentialism, he prefers to use the very special term *Existenzphilosophie* as best descriptive of his own philosophy. And even that term, if used in a restrictive sense, he regards as misleading; its main function being rather to distinguish "primordial, eternal philosophy" from the professional, academic philosophy of university teachers. Whereas the latter, as Jaspers sees it, tend to regard philosophy as a sort of intellectual exercise, too often degenerating into a duel of wits, in which the issues are largely verbal, and which, whatever the outcome, has no profound effect on their actual lives, he for his part holds to the conviction "that genuine philosophizing must well up from a man's individual existence and address itself to other individuals, to help them to achieve [their] true existence."[1] To be genuine, a man's philosophy must be inseparable from the man himself, not merely a "way of life," but very life itself, not a mere doctrine or theory, but somehow a transcending of all set doctrines and all mere theories. Only in and by philosophizing, rather than in a claim to knowledge, does the "historically concrete existence of the individual"—a favorite phrase—realize itself.

In an article "On My Philosophy" by Jaspers, included in Kaufmann's book[2] the author briefly presents his estimate of the significance of the history of philosophy for philosophy as such. As he sees it,

> Logic and the history of philosophy are complementary. . . . What is being developed there [in history] as the world of thought, is demonstrated here [in logic] as the reality of thought.

The history of thought as generally understood, however, is far from what Jaspers has in mind. No doubt that history is today more completely and more profoundly comprehended, as a chronologically and to some extent logically ordered series of "doctrines" than ever before. In the Western world, at least, every individual philosopher of the past has been subjected to exhaustive and thoroughgoing studies, and his place in western thought has been specified with painstaking accuracy, his special contribution made plain for all to recognize. But at the same time this very thorough knowledge of the history of philosophy has brought to light the contrast between "mere knowing about doctrines" and history, and "life itself"—"actually believed truth." And this contrast has led to serious questions as to "the ultimate sense of this tradition, great as the tradition is, and despite all the satisfaction it has provided and still provides today." In short "we question whether the truth of philosophizing has been grasped, or even if it can be grasped in this tradition." The history of philosophy appears to be one thing, and philosophy as such quite another thing. In Jaspers' opinion, even Hegel's bold identification of the two failed, in the long run, basically to alter this rather general way of thinking.

What has happened to bring about such a state of affairs?

Among other influential factors, Jaspers cites the "destruction of all authority," a "radical disillusionment in an overconfident reason," and the gradual breakdown of all the old bonds between members of the western community. As a result, the life has departed from the old "words and doctrines," and the conviction is growing that "philosophizing, to be authentic, must grow out of our new reality and there take its stand."[3] Contemporary philosophy looks more and more to Kierkegaard and Nietzsche for guidance, and this means, among other things, a wholly new intellectual attitude. No such systems of thought as are found in traditional philosophy, no fixed doctrine or requirement, but rather a most radical and thoroughgoing opposition to "mere reason," is what stands out in their writings. Not to be misunderstood as hostility to reason, what these men teach is rather an "attitude in the medium of infinite reflection . . . which is conscious of being unable to attain any real ground by itself."[4] Such a ground, Jaspers is convinced, is to be found only "in the depths of *Existenz.*" Thus reflection must become "self-reflection," and the thinker must realize that "the way to truth is through understanding oneself," through "an inner act of the entire man; the bringing forth of oneself out of possibilities in thought so as to apprehend Being in empirical existence."[5]

Taken by themselves, these utterances are not very illuminating as to the content of the *Existenzphilosophie,* but perhaps they may serve to call attention to the spirit animating Jasper's thinking —his "philosophizing," as he likes to say. And after all, of a way of thinking which in a sense repudiates the very idea of a philosophical system, what can one do but try to convey something of its animating spirit?

Although, like many another thinker, "demanding the maximum of rationality" of the philosopher, it appears that something more than rationality— though a "more" which yet is not irrationality—is required in order to grasp the full meaning of *Existenz* as Jaspers strives to expound it. Above and beyond all intellectually constituted systems, *Existenz* points to "the problem of the clarification of the dark," "of what defies all determinate knowledge," and "the grasping of the bases out of which we live."[6]

Obviously it would require many pages to present an adequate exposition of the way in which Jaspers wrestles with what he regards as the basic problems confronting the contemporary philosopher. Many a student, indeed, might be inclined to relinquish the attempt to clarify further what seems on the face of it to defy all clarification, and might at this point feel himself justified in contending that in posing such a problem, the very terms in which it is formulated renders any intelligible solution of it impossible. In other words, it seems as if a demand is being made of philosophy which, if taken literally, in the very nature of the case cannot be met. Philosophy, as generally understood and pursued, makes its appeal to intelligibility, and to an intellectual comprehension of "the nature of things." For Jaspers, on the other hand, "philosophizing" means not alone this, but something more, something analogous to the spiritual communion, and even to the salvation of the religious man, as well. Perhaps, however, all that Jaspers has in mind might be regarded as a rather unfortunate way of calling attention to what some philosophers designate as a "sense of values"—a sense, namely, of moral, religious, and aesthetic issues, as well as of purely logical and epistemological ones.

However that may be, Jaspers is at any rate the author of extensive works, including one on the history of philosophy, which lend themselves as such to a critical examination in substantially the same way as do any other philosophical writings. And while such an examination runs the risk of violating what their author might well regard as the very spirit in which, and the very purpose for which they were written, it is also obvious that no other procedure is available to anyone other than a dedicated disciple of the Master.

II

Fortunately, so far as the history of philosophy in particular is concerned, it requires no more effort of the student to decipher Jaspers' conception of its role in relation to philosophy as such, than in the case of the other thinkers whose doctrines have already been examined. For this purpose, in addition to the brief work included in Kaufmann's volume, the first volume of *Die Grossen Philosophen*[7] must be studied. And mention should also be made of separate works on *Nietzsche*[8] and *Descartes*;[9] the former serving as a sort of introduction to Jaspers' own thinking, the latter to the revelation of such "typically modern errors" as the "mistaking of speculative thought for rationally cogent insight" and the "inversion of modern science" which has dogged the progress of science from the very beginning.[10] In view of the importance attributed by Jaspers to the history of philosophy, it is surprising to find so little attention paid to it, however, in the volume entitled *The Philosophy of Karl Jaspers*.[11]

What, then, is the very special meaning which Jaspers attaches to philosophy in its historical dimension, and what corresponding mode of exposition does he consider best fitted to render that meaning?

In the "Essay on My Philosophy" included in Kaufmann's volume, Jaspers outlines his program.

> In my Universal History of Philosophy [he explains] I aim to present historically known philosophizing without chronological order, but as the one great phenomenon, always coherent in itself, of the revelation of Being in humanity; how from its roots (in China, India, Greece) it developed in great cycles, constantly conditioned by sociological circumstances and psychological events, in relation to science and religion, and echoing art and poetry; how it strives toward a single great, organized unity of opposites, which at the boundaries, fail to yield solutions in Time, and, in failing, bring to awareness the truth of Transcendent Being.[12]

But as Jaspers is quick to recognize, to lay out such a program is one thing, and actually to carry it out is another. All that the individual historian, with his limited powers and insight, can accomplish is to work at the immense task, leaving it to his successors to carry it further, and to improve what has already been done. It should be noted, however, that these qualifications, in spite of their commonplace appearance and terminology, have their own peculiar meaning in the context to which they apply. For the task itself, as Jaspers conceives it, is definitely not that of the conventional historian—so much, at least, is already obvious. Such key phrases as "the revelation of Being in humanity," and the long concluding one, however obscure their meaning at this stage, certainly show clearly enough that in this view the history of philosophy is in some basic sense inseparable from "philosophizing" in the present. What actually amounts to nothing less than a repudiation of conventional historical writings, and, positively speaking, an entirely novel and profoundly important reading of philosophy's history, is what Jaspers is plainly leading the student to expect.

In the Preface and long Introduction to Volume I of *Die Grossen Philosophen*, Jaspers goes to great lengths to spell out in copious detail his conception of his undertaking as already outlined. His mode of exposition is such that it requires considerable repetition of central ideas in different contexts in order to reveal their full and special import, and accordingly the student seeking to understand that work must resign himself to a similar procedure.

Conceding that Hegel was the first to conceive of a truly universal history of philosophy, he nevertheless naturally failed to see something that has become more and more obvious with the passage of time since Hegel's pioneering efforts. The essential meaning of philosophy's history is not to be brought out simply by presenting a sort of representation or running account of philosophy's past, after the manner appropriate to the history of science, say, or in terms of any sort of dialectical formula, à la Hegel, and viewed as comprising a unitary and complete process. For the contemporary thinker, as Jaspers sees it, there is no such unitary process. And even if there were, to grasp it as such would presuppose the ability somehow to stand outside and above it. (Recall Dilthey's claim, and Collingwood's repudiation of the claim, to be able thus to stand above the course of history.) Hence, for such a thinker, recognizing that this ability is not given to the historian, the only alternative is to conceive of himself as *an active participant* in history.

That being so, and even tacitly recognized as so by many actual historians, the only practical way to study history has hitherto seemed to be by means of specific presuppositions and goals. And this means that definite *aspects* of the history of philosophy, turn and turn about, have been methodically emphasized.

The five aspects or points of view which Jaspers finds have either singly or in various combinations characterized histories of philosophy so far, are: (1) the simply or naively historical (i.e., chronological, geographical, sociological, "spirit-of-the-age," etc., interpretations); (2) the factual (i.e., the problems and their solutions, the systems of thought in abstraction from the temporal order); (3) the genetic (the derivation of philosophy from its 'sources' in myth, religion, language, etc., etc.); (4) the practical or pragmatic (application or realization of philosophy in the actual life of peoples and periods); and (5) the dynamic (the endless strife and conflict of minds, in which even the contemporary philosopher participates). Readers can see for themselves that this description does indeed rather exhaustively cover such historical writings as they are familiar with.

Yet there is no such thing as a synthesis of these aspects possible in practice, even if projected ideally in theory. For any such pretended synthesis would itself inevitably presuppose either a definite and hence biased point of view, or an unjustifiable claim somehow to be able to transcend the entire historical order, and take up a stand outside of it, which is—to repeat—manifestly impossible.

No; a thorough grasp of these aspects, even if taken together, *so far as may be*, is just a necessary prerequisite to fulfilling the task of the historical thinker who is at the same time philosophizing in his own right, as Jaspers envisages him. Like all history, the final aim of the history of philosophy is "existential historical consciousness," or individuality self-conscious in its historical determination.

That is to say, to the extent that great individual thinkers become actually present in one's own conscious being, all those 'aspects' as it were fade into the background. Conditioned though they admittedly are in those five ways, such personages yet become "timeless objective figures," transcending their age, while at the same time expressive of it. And incidentally this idea, of what may be called a kingdom of great thinkers, does away with the possibility of basing one's own thinking upon the philosophy of a single thinker, however profound and compelling his thought may be.

There is no such thing as "the absolute truth" embodied in any one man, age, or place; surely if it teaches nothing else, history teaches at least that much. Moreover, the demand is, or at any rate should be, so far as history is concerned, insistent, to come to know and appreciate even that which repels intellectually; to *love,* not only what attracts but also what is foreign to one, what appears as sheer intellectual perversity, as well as what has a natural affinity with one's own intellectual tendencies and interests.

As true, and as trite as it may be, that no one individual can fully realize the ideal goal of adequately presenting the one and only account of these exceptional personages it is also true that the ordinary thinker must (and can) do his best to immerse himself in their lives and works, for only in that way can he realize his own more modest potentialities. Though scientific objectivity is neither possible nor even desirable where the history of philosophy is concerned, one can listen to, and learn from, these Great Ones, and so come to love and participate in the society of the best and highest among mankind. And in this wise, and in this wise only, one becomes historically actual in his own right, consciously aware of the potentialities of his own existence.

Thus, as Jaspers sees it, his task is to assume the entire burden of so presenting "the great philosophers" as to bring out more clearly than ever before precisely wherein their greatness consists, and consequently to show how, in their uniqueness, in their very presence on this earth, they speak to him who has ears to hear, and may even enter into the very existence of whoever has made the necessary effort to nourish himself out of their greatness.

But just at this point at least two critical questions arise. How are the *great* thinkers to be distinguished from their lesser brethren? And to what sort of organization, for purposes of exposition (the simple chronological order having been abandoned), is it legitimate and instructive to expose these great ones?

In reply to the first question Jaspers establishes certain specific criteria of greatness. As he clearly recognizes, application of these criteria is essential if sheer arbitrariness is to be avoided. But ever since the time of the ancient philosophers, and especially in the last two centuries, philosophy has assumed the character of a Science, i.e., logical form and system. But this standard has recently been seriously questioned. One extreme—that of logistic and positivistic "science" has rejected metaphysics and all that had previously been regarded as philosophy. The other extreme view has adopted a hostile attitude to science, exploiting instead the penetrating powers of language.

The point is that none of these alternatives recognizes greatness as a mark of philosophy. On the one hand, it is held that philosophy in the proper sense of the word began only in the late nineteenth century, while on the other hand, concentration on the *scientific* character of philosophy has destroyed the very seriousness of philosophy as such.

In spite of these aberrations (as Jaspers regards them), however, the great philosophers have somehow acquired and preserved a consciousness of the basic problems of human existence, of the world, of being, and of Deity. They continue to illuminate, beyond all limited goals, the course of life in general, to wrestle with questions of human limitations, and to strain after the unlimited, the all-encompassing. The essence of philosophy thus clearly appears as universality, a striving to gain an ever clearer idea of "the whole."

And finally a great philosopher is one who has a profound sense of normative values, not acquired and transmitted by sheer power of authority but by inducing the thinker to listen, to convince himself, and to bring others to rise to their own personal insights. As distinguished from organized religion, the normative impulse in philosophy displays itself in the freedom of the individual thinker, and as distinguished from objective science, philosophizing, by the exercise of what Jaspers calls "philosophical faith" centers its attention on the essential self-being of humanity.

As far as the history of philosophy is concerned, however, greatness has become as it were absorbed or obscured, under the sheer encyclopedic weight of the vast number of names with which that history has encumbered itself. History as usually presented has become primarily a means of informing oneself of those countless individual philosophers, without distinction, who belong to the ever increasing list. Under such conditions, history comprises either an endless series of mere names, or a more or less arbitrary selection of outstanding thinkers, differing assignments of rank, and various groupings or classifications. No historical judgments can be accepted as definitive, and all remains subject to constant revision.

In the nineteenth century, for example, Pascal was rated as an aphorist; Kierkegaard at the beginning of the twentieth century was scarcely recognized at all; while Nietzsche was described as a poet. Yet today these three men are taken most seriously. And so the pendulum of ordinary history incessantly swings from one standard of estimation to another.

Thus the insistent and all-important questions arise—what are the considerations which may lead to the determination of greatness, order of rank, and grouping? How is one to select and group the great thinkers, and what is the philosophical significance, if any, of such selection and grouping?

One might answer that the historical consciousness[13] is able to order philosophers of the past in their respective periods, and in terms of their various interrelations with each other—cooperative, antithetical, or developmental as the case may be, e.g., Socrates, Plato, Aristotle; Descartes, Spinoza, Leibniz; Locke, Berkeley, Hume; Kant, Fichte, Schelling, Hegel. But something is inevitably lost in the process. The individual philosophers are so extraordinarily different, that they first reveal themselves fully only when they are as it were lifted out of their historical contexts. Kant, for example, presents a philosophical personality totally unlike that of the others in the above list, while Fichte, Schelling and Hegel are among themselves very heterogeneous in their basic natures. And, on the contrary, groupings which can be justified neither on chronological nor on any of the other customary historical grounds (to say nothing of extraneous psychological grounds), such as a common set of problems, may yet reveal a more profound kinship in "the eternal kingdom of great spirits."

In order to bring to light this profound spiritual kinship, however, the historian has no other resources available than are afforded by such criteria as concern with profound philosophical problems, the manner in which fundamental insights are acquired, the way of comprehending the meaning of human life in its innermost reaches, and the type of spiritual activity displayed in actual sociological concerns.

III

Applying these criteria, Jaspers forms three main groups of "great philosophers," each dealing with three or more individuals, or even divisible into three or more sub-groups. And to digest such a large mass of material Jaspers has projected no less than three very large volumes, of which only the first (of 956 pages) has so far been published.

The first main group includes men who through their very existence and personalities have influenced incomparably the entire subsequent course of human history—the four standard-bearers, as it were, of all humanity: Socrates, Buddha, Confucius, and Jesus. Although one may hesitate to call them all philosophers, and though only one (Confucius) was a writer, they manifestly have an extraordinary meaning for philosophy, and they tower above all others in their eternal significance.

The second main group includes all those great thinkers who are usually and unquestionably counted among the philosophers. Jaspers here establishes four sub-groups, namely, (2a), the foundation-layers for constructive thinking—Plato, St. Augustine, Kant; (2b), metaphysicians proper (e.g., Parmenides, Heracleitus . . . Spinoza, Lao-tse . . .; (2c), the great uprooters, and negatively inclined thinkers (Abelard, Descartes, Hume), and the radical awakeners (Pascal, . . . Kierkegaard, Nietzsche); and (2d), the creative systematizers Aristotle, Thomas Aquinas, Hegel, *et al.*).

In general, this second grouping issues in a selection of outstanding thinkers, such as would be included in any concise history of philosophy, and such as might be arranged in various groups and sub-groups depending on some more or less plausible principle of arrangement.

Lastly, the third main group includes all those scientists, poets, artists, humanists, statesmen, *et al.*, who had philosophical interests, or who indirectly, at least, strongly influenced the course of philosophical speculation.

Of course no one historian can fully master the vast and complicated "web of history," and it is inevitable that some worthy thinkers will be slighted, and that any sort of grouping and any principles of selection are bound to be to some extent arbitrary. But what is to Jaspers the inherently significant presupposition upon which his groupings are based, is that of "a manifold of personal structures in their

essential interconnections." Instead of what he regards as a crudely factual orientation in space-time,
he envisages an orientation in "personal space."
What becomes most clear, however, to Jaspers himself, largely as a direct result of this very mode of
presentation, is that every great thinker overleaps
any and every classification by virtue of his uniqueness, his irreplaceability, and his solitary grandeur.
In the last analysis, therefore, each individual must
be dealt with as if in complete independence of
his fellows. No order imposed upon these Great
Ones can be of a strictly logical sort; rather the
order must derive, as it were, from insight into
that which concretely constitutes each individual
historical case. (Incidentally, this acute observation obviously is directly pertinent to the classifications proposed by Renouvier and Dilthey.) The
very historicity of things defies complete absorption in, or subsumption under any set of universals or generalities—in short, any and every sort
of classification.

Thus this ordering into groups is designed
only to bring out as clearly as possible the presence
of something universal, immanent in each individual, and thus to reveal the essential two-sidedness
of philosophy—the individual and the universal—
to its fullest extent. When the philosopher carries
on his philosophizing in the context of the history
of philosophy, as thus conceived, according to
Jaspers, he will both comprehend the world of
philosophers as a whole, and at the same time be
sensible of the uniqueness of each historically conditioned personage. Above all, the historian must

beware of construing the temporal course of philosophy either in terms of antithetical conflicts, i.e., affirmations and negations,[14] or of evolutionary developments and "influences." For in one and the same thinker antithetical forces are often at work; and such general concepts as "development" and "influence" can only serve the illegitimate purpose of subsumption and classification. It is true, of course, that knowing other philosophers enables one to know any one great thinker better. Also, the historian who meets and "lives with" the Great Ones of history, and includes or excludes certain individuals from his purview, thus exercises his choices, and thereby realizes his own freedom as a philosopher. Such choices determine the range of possibilities open to his personal philosophizing. And the author of a book like that of Jaspers has the welcome task of providing clues to the reader for making his choices, in his turn.

The reader, for his part, should of course never rest satisfied with mere "philological-historical" information and learning, however complete and even profound it may be. For it is a mark of the great thinker that he is always contemporary, that he transcends time, and that he opens up possibilities to be realized by those who become acquainted with his accomplishments.

Philosophy and humanity are so closely intertwined that the personality of the thinker becomes as it were an integral part of an account of his philosophy (cf. Renouvier and Dilthey). And even those thinkers who display hostility toward each other can yet be taken up into the general nexus of communication; for by one's very intellectual and spiritual antipathies one gains further insight into the nature of philosophy itself.

There is indeed something which is ready to respond, in any man, to the appearance of Greatness, in whatever form. As a "possible *Existenz*" one hears whatever philosopher speaks to him out of his *Existenz,* and the method or methods by which this truly spiritual communication comes about is a function of the communication itself—something which is rather the meaning of all methods of philosophical study than any one method as such. Thus the basic actuality of philosophy's history is just the presence in it of the great thinkers who provide the essential impetus of future generations, and the substance upon which those generations nourish themselves. But unlike science, with its impartial, impersonal objectivity of knowledge, and its consequent independence of the individual scientist, philosophical doctrines are the only means whereby the personal formulations of the individual thinker gain universality; one must think oneself into the worlds of thought of the philosophers themselves, in their inseparability from distinct philosophical personalities. And although from an empirico-historical point of view great thinkers are representatives of their times, they yet have a unique status and overleap all ages. The historical position and the temporal interconnection of philosophies and philosophers is at best only a preliminary to comprehending them in their trans-historical reality. In actuality, the great philosophers cannot be cabined and confined in a mere temporal series;

they participate in no sheerly logical process of development, but are rather members of a spiritual community, all of whom communicate with each other and with all other men.[15] Unlike great scientists, great philosophers do not in their works offer "proofs" and demonstrations of objective knowledge (even when they ostensibly claim to do so), but are rather pathfinders who point the way to all future generations of men. Science is the realm of pure intellects, of "consciousness in general," whereas philosophy is the realm of complete human beings, who "live and move and have their being" in thought-comprehended existence. Philosophical thinking is thinking inseparably bound up with concrete human situations, with human choices and decisions. In his work the philosopher lives, and the meaning of his unique existence is an integral part of his concern.

Just here one must not mistakenly apply the test as to whether a man practices what he preaches, for such a test would presuppose a doctrine, a set of formulas on the one hand, and on the other, an individual measured juristically against that doctrine. Rather, the truth of his philosophy is one and the same as the spiritual integrity of the philosopher. Psychology is unable to penetrate this unity; understanding here gives way to a sort of comprehension of the unique human existence which yet has a universal import, and personal communication is the only means to attain this comprehension.[16]

But no life, no existence is without its inner conflicts; in intellectual terms no thinker is entirely consistent with himself. Such contradictions, however, are not always a sign of defects. As Nietzsche (and others) noted, a very good measure of the great thinker is just the range of contradictions his speculations encompass. Moreover, in original philosophizing elements are interconnected, which *subsequently* become quasi-independent, so that looking backward they come to be viewed abstractly as standing in opposition to each other. This very fate has overtaken even such Great Ones as Socrates, Plato, Kant, and Jesus.

IV

In the closing pages of his long introduction to *Die Grossen Philosophen,* Jaspers sums up the problems and aims of his book. Paradoxically, while presenting his heroes in an historical context, and arranging them in groups, the ultimate aim is to see them as trans-historical figures, contemporary with all times, and as unique individuals. The groupings do indeed bring out one important point, namely that throughout the entire history of philosophy a ceaseless struggle goes on, evident in conflicts of ideas and theories, but a struggle which yet reveals a special sort of spiritual kinship and interrelation among all philosophers.

A second aim which Jaspers keeps before him is to reveal the essential unity of philosophy, in spite of its extremely rich diversity, rather than to rest satisfied with the superficial appearance of a contingent manifold of opinions, with no truth in them, and of a game-like character. Indeed, the very exposition itself claims to be not so much a sheer objective presentation,—something impossible in the nature of the case—as a search for truth in its turn. This it *must* and *can* be, Jaspers holds, and indeed this is the only genuine *raison d'être* of such a work.

But—to repeat—the search must be carried on neither from some assumed position of superiority over all history, nor, at the opposite extreme, as an exercise in polemics aimed at belittling one or all of the great thinkers, but rather as a *critical attempt at communication,* with a view to deriving something from each individual by means of which to unite them all.

In short, historical knowledge is realized only in and by its assimilation in one's own *Existenz.* The history of philosophy is in its own right an essential moment of philosophy, of philosophizing, and the more closely the historian draws to the historical actuality, the more is he himself a philosopher engaging in his own philosophizing.

Jaspers furthermore claims for his book that it has been written to be understood without requiring of the reader that he first learn a definite philosophy as a clue to that understanding.

Above all, Jaspers has broken deliberately with all customary modes of presentation of the material. For as he sees it, in the society of philosophers, one must present each one in his uniqueness, and all, in their marvelous diversity, as directed toward, not a single outcome, but as a continuous and continuing presence of the whole. The whole truth is embodied only in the unity of time and eternity rather than in either one alone. Mere temporality is a mere coming and going, and mere eternity is an unreal abstraction. One must therefore aim at combining the temporally empirical, with, and en-lightened by the transempirical, so as to reveal the individual thinker in his historical context, but as nevertheless a spokesman for, a representative of the super-historical Truth.

This super-historical Truth is not the same as objective knowledge, akin to that acquired by scientific methods, but is rather a kind of insight peculiar to philosophy, and embodied, however imperfectly, in one's own philosophizing. Included in this insight is a lively sense of historicity, a basic condition of human existence, with its irrevocable past, and its future pregnant with possibilities in terms of which man realizes his freedom.

Though Jaspers is certainly not the first thinker to emphasize the personal character of philosophy, as contrasted with the impersonality characteristic of science, the specific meaning he attaches to it is uniquely his own. Philosophy, for him, supplants organized religion (which helps to explain why he includes Jesus and Buddha among *Die Grossen Philosophen*), and what he calls "philosophical faith" is inherent in his philosophizing.

Holding to such principles inevitably makes for a certain elusiveness in Jaspers' position; he is not to be caught in any of the usual nets philosophers endeavor to snare their opponents in. With re-spect to the history of philosophy in particular, what distinguishes Jaspers' treatment of it from all others, is not so much anything unusual in his expositions and interpretations of the doctrines of the philosophers included in his account, as what he counsels his readers to make out for themselves from that history with the assistance he is able to afford them. Following Jaspers' directions and expositions, one will become acquainted with the gist of each thinker's work, and will presumably thereupon proceed to acquaint himself at first hand with the principal works of those thinkers themselves.

So far, this is the kind of service any historian would be expected to render. In so far as the chronological order is violated by Jaspers in his groupings, this might be taken as no more than an attempt, by one historian among others, to present the history of philosophy in a more significant manner (in some sense) than sheer chronology provides. As noted before, other groupings are certainly possible, and even, on Jaspers' own showing, quite permissible. For in the end what he constantly insists upon is above all else the reader's gradually coming to realize the unique fashion in which each individual great thinker "communicates" with other philosophers, including the reader himself, in the course of his philosophizing. It is a sort of spiritual transaction, and the result to be anticipated is a more profound and comprehensive insight into human *Existenz,* as experienced by each individual for himself. This insight, indeed, is what Jaspers calls "philosophical truth." The sheer temporal succession of philosophers becomes less and less important, while at the same time the inherent historicity of man's situation becomes only the more evident. The student of the history of philosophy thus immerses himself, as it were, in the inseparable unity of the man-in-his-work, and gains the spiritual insight which comes from this continuing communion of all philosophers throughout the ages.

Such is the spirit in which Jaspers envisions the task of the historian of philosophy, and what he conceives to be the outcome of its study.

And it is almost a platitude among devoted historians that in some very general sense these prescriptions are perfectly acceptable. In that sense, all historians can and do observe them. But there is more at stake here than may be evident at first glance. For what distinguishes this philosopher's rendering of the history of philosophy from all others, may be put in the form of a paradox—the paradox, namely that for him history, as commonly understood, is not his concern at all!

This point may perhaps be best established and clarified by means of an example. In Jaspers' real grasp and clear exposition of Kant there is included only the sparsest reference to his predecessors; practically none, in fact, to the basic conflict between empiricism and rationalism, which Kant certainly sought persistently to wrestle with and to resolve. But how can Kant's work be understood and justly evaluated without extensive reference to this conflict? And this sort of neglect of important "influences" on the course of Kant's own thinking is characteristic, and, indeed, deliberate. Actuated by his commendable aim to present Kant-in-his-work, in his uniqueness, and in his everlasting significance for philosophy, Jaspers has nevertheless omitted from his exposition and interpretation an essential portion of what one needs to know in order to attain a true sense of Kant's originality and philosophical genius. In thus *isolating* Kant, with a view to realizing his laudable purpose, Jaspers has actually to a considerable extent defeated this very purpose. However outstanding the philosopher and his philosophy, he is yet, as Jaspers himself on occasion allows, circumscribed by his setting in time and place, and as one man among others; and largely to disregard reference to this inevitable limitation and to these conditions, is not to bring clearly to the fore precisely wherein Kant's greatness lies.

And so of any other great philosopher. Disregard of chronological considerations, carried to the extent to which Jaspers carries it, in considerable part robs his readers of an absolutely essential perspective. So that while one may profit greatly from Jaspers' work, and fully acknowledge the value of the insights he affords, one nevertheless is forced to conclude that he has not produced a *history of philosophy* in the real sense of the word.

And why could not all that Jaspers actually achieves by his groupings equally well be achieved within the context of more usual modes of exposition, plus the undeniable advantages attaching to such a customary procedure? Those characteristics which Jaspers attaches to Kant's philosophy, for example, which it shares with the philosophies of such and such other thinkers, and which therefore induces Jaspers to group Kant with those others in a non-temporal order, could all be noted in the course of any ordinary history of philosophy.

Is it not evident, all too evident, that in the last analysis the basic reason why Jaspers insists on his unusual groupings is precisely because they enable him to ignore the only things which historians usually (and surely rightly!) stress, e.g., influences, development of lines of thought, and in general all the complex interrelations of philosophical theories with each other? And this procedure, in turn, serves the specific and all important purpose of enabling Jaspers to interpret all past philosophy as implying or illustrating and ultimately confirming his own personal conception of philosophizing.

This sharp criticism may however strike the reader as unfairly captious. Valid on the formal, verbal level as it may be, it yet ignores the whole animating spirit of the *Existenzphilosophie*—so the sympathetic reader might protest. Philosophical truth, in the view of the author of that philosophy, is less a matter of formal consistency, and primarily, rather, a matter of spiritual value (cf. Croce!). Formal consistency is abstract, and places a premium on sheer logical rigor, at the expense of profound spiritual insight. Like the reliance of religion on faith, by the sincerely devout, in spite of inconsistencies in doctrine, dogma or creed—in short, in all verbal formulations—just so *Existenzphilosophie*, for Jaspers, is adherence to "philosophical faith" eluding and transcending, in his view, any merely verbal statement. And like the "communion of saints" the "communication" of philosophers with each other is a matter of spiritual co-existence and kinship of which words are instrumentalities of somewhat limited effectiveness.

Ah, yes, replies the critic, now at last Jaspers is clearly unmasked; he is indeed making a religion of his philosophy! And however highly one may admire spiritual fervor, and even though it be granted that it, or something closely resembling it, is essential to philosophical greatness, still the task of philosophy is and must be carefully distinguished from the role of religion.

The proper, the sole task of philosophy is to understand; its main appeal *must be* to the intellect; and this involves strict adherence to logical principles. Truth *is* a spiritual value; but the criteria of truth are one thing, and the spiritual value realized in religious devotion is another thing.

Such is, in substance, the drift of comments by such well-informed students of the *Existenzphilosophie* as Walter Kaufmann,[17] and of several of the contributors to the Schilpp volume on Jaspers.

So far as these comments are justified—and a re-reading, in their light, of the preceding pages is instructive—the significance attributed by Jaspers to his version of the history of philosophy in relation to his own "philosophizing" becomes that much clearer and greater. In his mind, evidently, the two are inseparable; the entire history of philosophy is but the other side, as it were, of his own philosophy, seen in temporal perspective, and in its various aspects. *All* philosophy, no matter how conceived or pursued by its practitioners, is really a more or less implicit or explicit process of "philosophizing" as Jaspers understands it; that is what alone gives to philosophy, in his view, its profound meaning and value.

Once again the history of philosophy—to adapt a well-known Kantian phrase—is treated as a means to the historian's own ends, which he uncritically identifies with the import of philosophy in general.

Thus it still remains the case that the demand is still to be fully met for a rendering of that history which shows it to be somehow relevant to all philosophy, to the most diverse contemporary philosophical theories just as they stand, and not as re-interpreted by another philosopher, and not to just one among them all—least of all to just one!

Or is this a demand that cannot, in the nature of the case, be fully met? Perhaps, after all, Jaspers has come as near—nearer than most if not all other thinkers!—to realizing in practice what in theory he may be said to teach, but what must forever remain only an ideal goal, never more than very imperfectly to be reached by any one philosopher turned historian of his own subject.

In the last two chapters of this study, following a brief glance at certain other recent accounts of the meaning of the history of philosophy for philosophy itself, this last possibility will be considered a little further.

6. *BERGSON, GILSON, RUSSELL:*
INTUITION AND DOGMATISM

It cannot be said that any other recent or contemporary philosophers have pondered so deeply, or given so much attention to "a central philosophical problem," as Professor Murphy called it, "concerning the historicity of a philosophy which is nevertheless not history," as have the thinkers already included in this study.

True, on the continent of Europe, in France, Italy and Germany, there is manifest a continuing lively interest in the problem.

In Italy, the *Rivista della historia della filosofia,* and studies such as Mario del Pra's recent *La Storiografica filosofica antica*[1] witness to this interest. In France, occasional articles appear in philosophical periodicals, not indeed on the general problem—which is seemingly assumed somehow to have been solved—but on various details, mainly technical in nature, and on side issues connected with it; and such recent monographs as E. Bréhier's *La philosophie et son passé,*[2] and H. Gouhier's *L'histoire et sa philosophie*[3] perform the same service on a somewhat larger scale. In Germany also one may confi-

dently expect to come across articles and monographs
similar in nature to those in France and Italy.

But elsewhere, if Marxism be excluded on the
ground that it is concerned only incidentally with
the history of philosophy and primarily with quite
a different thing, namely the so-called philosophy of
history, and in Britain and America in particular,
the spirit of the age can almost be described as anti-
historical, so far as philosophy is concerned.

All the same, certain examples of the modicum
of interest displayed recently in France and Britain,
by leading philosophers, are sufficiently important
and revealing to warrant brief consideration here,
and at this point.

I

It would certainly seem reasonable, a priori, to
anticipate that one who throughout his long and
noteworthy philosophical career preached the doctrine of taking time seriously, would above all
others stress the inherent significance for philosophy of its history. But when one actually turns
to the pages of Henri Bergson's various works, such
anticipations find little in the way of confirmation.

In his most widely celebrated work, *Creative
Evolution*, the author presents a brief study of
certain past systems of philosophy, mainly in order,
as he says, "to define more clearly in its opposition
to others, a philosophy which sees in duration the
very stuff of reality." But in a less widely known
"Lecture"[4] on "Philosophical Intuition," Bergson
envisages the history of philosophy more as a prob-

lem in its own right. To create a living philosophy, he here asserts, the philosopher must join battle with his predecessors, as well as with his contemporaries, and, in a sense, even with human nature in general.

According to Bergson's well-known doctrine, "Intuition" is the philosophical mind at its creative best, and the exercise of this intuitive grasp of reality makes its debut, in joining the battle, with a resounding "No." The first step of a genuinely creative philosopher, especially since he is bound to be a bit uncertain of himself at this early stage, *must be* definitely to reject various theories and doctrines upheld as certainties by other thinkers.

But this is only the first step. The next step, the decisive, constitutive one, is an equally resounding "yes," a very positive affirmation. For if intuition be indeed the correct designation for philosophical thinking, dialectic, Bergson holds, is so to speak its language. As he had already explained in *Creative Evolution*,[5] "dialectic is necessary to put intuition to the proof; necessary also in order that intuition should break itself up into concepts and so be propagated to other men. . ." And again, "dialectic is what insures the agreement of our thought with itself." But alas!, by this "relaxation of intuition," "many different agreements are possible, while there is only one truth."

The one intuitive insight, the one vision, which is all that is vouchsafed to any, even the most creative philosopher, is something the description of which well-nigh overleaps all the resources of even this dialectical language. Less a vision than a con-

tact which generates an impulsion, an impulsion
which is more a movement than a direction—such are
the phrases which tumble over each other on Bergson's lips in his effort to express the verbally in-
expressible. The impulsion, the spiritual energy,
one may perhaps suppose, exerted by the creative
thinker, manifests itself in, or as, the dialectical ten-
sion between the "no" and the "yes" in the philosophical advance which gives a genuinely new direction to the thought of the past. (Is there not a
definite echo of Renouvier in this conception of dialectic?) Thus a new thought develops out of the soil
of past thoughts, much as does the seed or cell of
a plant out of its earthen soil, into further and
further sub-divisions and ramifications of itself.
These germinating thoughts find expression in
words; and that means, of course, in a pre-existing
medium—a medium never designed to give expression to just these thoughts. But the philosopher may
choose almost arbitrarily the first elements of this
medium, provided only that the other elements are
complementary to them. Thus what is essentially
the same thought can be expressed in diverse phrases
composed of different words, provided only that
these words give expression to the same dialectical
relationships.

Such, as Bergson sees it, are the psychological and
linguistic aspects of the process by which a new philosophy develops, and finally, in its turn dies away.
With the passage of time the language employed
by the philosopher comes more and more to supplant, instead of expressing thought. Too often, for
example, in expounding the thoughts of other phi-

losophers of the past or present, a mere repetition of the words usurps the place that should be occupied with an effective and sympathetic immersion in the thoughts themselves.[6] This inevitable ossification of language, in the form of verbal formulas and labels, repeated *ad nauseam,* favors the delusion that there are certain perennial problems of philosophy, ever recurring, and in this wise transcending time. But even granting that the verbal formulation remains the same, the meaning conveyed by it may vary as much as if the formulation itself had been radically altered. Whether this has actually happened or not, in any given case, is indeed one difficult question the conscientious historian has to face.

So far so good. In the light of the preceding, one might entertain some hope that Bergson would actually succeed, where others have failed, in formulating a tenable account of the relation of philosophy to its history. But both in his essay entitled *La pensée et le mouvant,* and in the article already cited on *Philosophical Intuition,* Bergson illustrates the doctrine just outlined in such a way as to show that important qualifications must attend any such hope.

If Plato, or Spinoza, or Berkeley had lived in other times than they actually did, Bergson explains, they would no doubt thereupon have formulated other theses than those they actually did formulate; but the movement or impulsion of their thoughts being the same, these theses would have taken on the same relationships to each other, like new words through which an old meaning continues to run. And consequently theirs would have been essentially the same philosophies as those to which they actually gave expression. In short, and as if in the utmost defiance of his own conception of "real duration" and of dialectic, the proper way to treat the thought of the past, Bergson holds, is to strive to recondense it, as it were, into its original intuitive vision, by following, in reverse order, the original "impulsion" in virtue of which the thinker expanded his intuition by means of dialectic and language. In this wise, and only so, the intuitive vision that was Plato's or Spinoza's or Berkeley's can be grasped —to the extent, that is, that the recondensation is effected in the mind of the historian. As if it were outside of time and history, as a sort of eternal essence, Bergson apparently conceives of each philosophical intuition as the intuition that it is, and in no way does or can it significantly "communicate"—to adapt Jaspers' language—with any other one. The only history of philosophy there is, or can be, on such a basis turns out to be a purely verbal and extraneous one. A philosophical system is, for Bergson, as acute critics have noted, closely analogous to a work of art, both in its uniqueness, and in its historical status with respect to other works or systems. (Though this comparison has not heretofore been drawn, there also seems to be an intriguing analogy between philosophical intuition in Bergsonian terms and Croce's aesthetic doctrine of "intuition-expression.")

There is such a contagious fervor characteristic of Bergson's writings, which even translation somehow partly preserves, that some readers are almost warmed to agreement, even in spite of their critical intellectual appraisal; and perhaps there is indeed enough truth, a near enough approach to truth in his doctrines, to justify a rather generous attitude toward them. In a later portion of this study, at all events, an attempt will be made to salvage what there seems to be the elements of truth in his reading of the history of philosophy.

In the meantime it becomes necessary briefly to outline quite a different conception of the role of philosophy's history with respect to philosophy itself.

II

No account, such as the present one, of how philosophers regard the history of their subject would be complete in the absence of some authoritative version by a representative of scholasticism or neo-scholasticism. In this connection the eminent neo-scholastic French philosopher Etienne Gilson at once comes to mind as a most suitable spokesman. His writings, both historical and expository, dealing with great thinkers of the past, and especially of the Middle Ages, have placed every other philosopher, whether interested in history or not, in his debt.

Most fortunately, Gilson is the author of a book, *The Unity of Philosophical Experience*,[7] in which he sets forth his reading of philosophy's history with his usual clarity and conciseness.

In that work he exhibits what he calls three typical "philosophical experiments," namely the medieval, the Cartesian, and the modern, each of which, in his view issues in a "breakdown," in

the form of either scepticism, positivism, materialism, or some such alleged philosophical malady.
On this view, the history of philosophy presents
the spectacle of many "blunders" or "failures," in-
termingled at sparse intervals with a few "successes."

The many failures are all due to a single basic
defect in metaphysics—in the shape either of the
adoption of erroneous metaphysical principles, or
in that of the misguided and self-defeating attempt
to eliminate metaphysics entirely. The few successes, on the other hand, are likewise all due to
a single basic intellectual virtue, namely a firm
grasp of the veritable "first principles," as Gilson
calls them, of all philosophy. And he concludes
his exposition by asserting that

> there is and there always will be a history of philos-
> ophy, because philosophy exists only in human minds,
> and because the world of knowledge and action . . .
> is a changing world, but there should be no history
> of the first principles themselves, because the meta-
> physical structure of reality itself does not change.[8]

This position he contrasts with historicism or
historical relativism[9]—the ephemeral realm of "contingent and irreversible facts" and of the non-
philosophical ideas of the special sciences. Truth
eternal (as embodied in orthodox neo-scholasticism)
triumphs over transitory error and the light of
"Perennis Philosophia" shines forth even in the
midst of historical gloom.

Such at least is the teaching of this particular work of its author, though it may not be as clearly maintained in other very valuable writings of his. At all events, the history of philosophy, interpreted in this way, is concerned only with what in the last analysis are superficial and external changes and details, while the eternal principles of "Pure Being" transcend time and change in their luminous self-certainty.

It may well have occurred to the critical reader of the preceding pages that one thing that is being illustrated beyond all shadow of doubt is a natural enough psychological characteristic of such outstanding philosophers as give some attention to the history of their subject. Whatever may be the philosophical significance of their reading of that history, *psychologically* it seems to be well demonstrated that creative ability, originality in philosophical thinking, is hardly consistent with the ability to construe the history of philosophy objectively; that is, in any other way than as more or less directly leading up to, preparing the way for their own personal speculations. The only question for which there is room in the minds of such creative thinkers seems to be whether *some* positive value may be accorded to that history in this respect, as is the case in several of the preceding instances, or whether history is simply to be looked upon as a record of more or less splendid failures, now at long last revealed for what they are, in order that philosophy may thereupon be set upon the right course to follow for evermore.

III

One final striking instance of the working of this psychological principle is afforded by the attitude of Bertrand Russell toward the history of philosophy. (The reader of course understands that nothing is implied, one way or the other, on the *philosophical* level, because of the influence of this principle.)

In his witty, entertaining, but too largely perverse *History of Western Philosophy,* Russell looks down, with a touch of venom not unmingled with patronizing superiority, on most of traditional philosophy. It seems that most philosophers in the past are guilty of such compounded intellectual crimes as confusion, sheer error, and downright sophistry, save only those select few who have recognized "logical analysis [as] the main business of philosophy," and who wisely use methods akin to those of science in that analysis. Though he does concede that there are "many things of great importance" which earlier philosophers have somehow brought to light almost in spite of themselves, and which "it would be too bad to forget or ignore," he yet considers that it is only in such works as *Principia Mathematica* and others inspired by it, or which may be viewed as partial anticipations of it, that philosophy has finally found the right path.

In such special studies as Hampshire's *Age of Reason,* Berlin's *The Age of the Enlightenment* (mostly on Hume's contribution to analytic philosophy) , and Morton White's *The Age of Analysis* (in which, paradoxically, more than half of the philosophers included are either opposed to the analytic way of "doing philosophy," or are not notable practitioners of it), the same general spirit and attitude seemingly animates the authors.

From a philosophical point of view (as distinct from the psychological), such leaders of one important contemporary line of thought seem to have reverted to a position not very different from that assumed by seveneenth century thinkers; mathematical certitude, scientific "rigor," and specific, limited goals, and the like, being prominent features of their philosophical program. And these tendencies are, of course, if not actively hostile, at least indifferent or unsympathetic toward any attempt to stress the historicity of philosophy. In a very real sense the "spirit" of much contemporary philosophy in English-speaking centers is thus anti-historical.

It still may be conceded, of course, if in a somewhat patronizing manner, that the study of philosophy in its historical dimension serves the purposes of general culture, and a fuller understanding of the past, and promotes broad-mindedness, tolerance, and other desirable characteristics—in short the purposes of a "general education"—very effectively. But this is far from entertaining the notion that "historicity" is an essential part or feature of philosophy as such; it may be in fact just a polite or indirect way of excluding it from the serious purview of the contemporary philosopher.

On the contrary, the view seems rather widely to prevail that those philosophers are substantially in the right who apply the Cartesian technique of doubting everything to all past philosophy; or else, to apply a metaphor of Locke's, regard the contemporary philosophical mind as a blank sheet of paper essentially unsullied by the speculations of the past, and invitingly ready to receive the impress of true and original thoughts. Scorning metaphysics, perhaps, resorting instead to scraps or phases of scientific procedures, or borrowing and adapting some scientific conception or theory, or utilizing theological dogmas or certain religious notions, appealing to the ineffable in the form of intuition or of an ultimate factuality, or for proposals for "doing philosophy" in terms of "language-games"—such are some of the subterfuges and devices employed by certain philosophers who seem unaware of any inherent resources which philosophy itself might bring to bear on its own distinctive problems, and whose last concern it is, seriously to wrestle with the question of determining the relation of philosophy to its history. The net result of these tendencies, characteristic to no inconsiderable degree, of contemporary British and American philosophy in particular, seems to be an ever closer and narrower concentration on very specific and even to a certain extent non-philosophical details and issues; and when history is taken into account at all it is only in a special case, or with reference to very special problems of one sort or another. As one unfortunate result of all this specialization, philosophers are well on the way to becoming completely unintelligible to each other, and each one largely engrossed only in his own pet interests.

One last comment on the content of this chapter. Looking back over these brief accounts of the way in which Gilson and Russell, respectively, view the history of philosophy, one may well be struck by the fact that their views, when directly confronted with each other, lend themselves very aptly to a Bergsonian interpretation. That is to say, each of these thinkers is possessed (in Bergsonian terms) of a single, unique "intuitive vision," formulated, it is true, in languages peculiar to each thinker, and verbally very different from each other, with ostensibly very diverse sets of dogmatically asserted "first principles"—principles embodying, on the one hand the metaphysics of Gilson's orthodox neo-scholasticism, and on the other hand the well-known "logical atomism" of Bertrand Russell—and issuing in very diverse lines of thought construed as rigorous deductions from those first principles. What might very appropriately be called—still in Bergsonian terms—the dialectical development of these two so superficially different lines of thought displays a remarkable parallelism when subjected to this sort of critical examination. And this parallelism, be it noted, extends even to their respective estimates of the largely negative significance which they attach to the history of philosophy for philosophy itself.

In short, the more fully the reader considers the matter, the more will he be struck by the singularly apt and as it were "made-to-order" illustrative value of this confrontation of two such widely opposed thinkers, an almost miraculous meeting of extremes which seems as if ideally designed in advance fully to confirm the Bergsonian doctrine. Or, if it be objected that "fully to confirm" is too strong a phrase, on the ground that a single instance is hardly enough to serve the purpose, at least it strongly suggests that there is some considerable element of validity in the doctrine.

In the next and concluding chapter of this study, this last comment will find a place in the general conclusions to which the whole study seems to lead.

What are the lessons that may be learned from this brief but fairly exhaustive review of the various ways in which philosophers have come to look upon the history of their subject, in relation to their own philosophical activities and interests?

On one extreme view, the history of philosophy is regarded as nothing but history, that is, a chronologically ordered record of the works, ideas, theories and systems produced by thinkers of the past; while at the same time philosophy *itself*—or more correctly, some particular contemporary philosophy viewing itself in that exalted fashion—seems determined to seek and find its justification in what amounts in principle to complete independence of its past (Gilson, Russell and others). That way lies a bold and unrepentant dogmatism, a supreme and uncritical self-assurance in some one set of basic "first principles."

At the other extreme, what may be called the historical dimension of philosophy assumes so dominant a role that hardly anything is left for philosophy to do but to become the humble handmaid of "the historical consciousness" (Dilthey, Croce, Collingwood). And that ways lies sheer historical relativism, and its almost inevitable correlate, namely scepticism.

In between these extremes it seems that practically every intermediate alternative has had its sponsors, including in this category those thinkers who naively enough presume to read all the diverse philosophies of the past in such a way as somehow to *lead up to* their own position now at long last presumed to be in some sense established definitively forevermore (Comte, Hegel (?), Jaspers, and others). Along these intermediate paths, a greater or lesser degree of critical appreciation for the accomplishments of earlier thinkers affords a valuable solace to the as yet uncommitted reader.

Meanwhile, histories of philosophy, if mainly of the text-book variety, continue to be written; and not a few of them measure up, to a reasonable degree, to the standards formulated by the late Professor Thilly in the Preface to his own work. As he saw it,

> a system of thought must be judged in the light of its own aims and historical setting, by comparison with the systems immediately preceding and following it, by its antecedents and results [and] by the development to which it leads.

Still keeping to generalities, it can indeed be asserted that even when history is written in the light of such extreme doctrines as those signalized above, it is nevertheless instructive and revealing, if in ways other than those explicitly intended by the writers. In spite of the very great abuses that may be inflicted upon it, and however distorted, one-sided, or prejudiced may be the standpoints of its practitioners, all history, and the history of philosophy in particular, has its uses, proves not to have been written entirely in vain. At the very worst, *how* history is written, in any given age, is, to future ages, a most useful and revealing indication of the character and ways of thinking of that age. How, in particular, any given philosopher views the philosophies of the past is intimately and inevitably bound up with his own way of carrying on philosophy, however original or novel his position may seem—however unhistorical or anti-historical at first glance. This statement holds true not only with respect to the individual philosopher's theories, but also with respect to his method or methods, with respect to his way of formulating the problems he undertakes to solve, and with respect both to the questions he raises and the answers he makes to those questions. Surely the evidence presented by the whole course of this present study, up to this point, amply suffices to establish this contention beyond any reasonable doubt.

Add to all this, as if to emphasize the importance of philosophy's history, even in an anti-historical age, the unequivocal statement by Jaspers that "philosophy is tested and characterized by the way in which it appropriates its history," and the equally striking assertion by Zeller, that "the more unintelligible we find the history of philosophy, the greater reason have we to doubt the truth of our own philosophic conceptions"; while, on the contrary, "the truer and more comprehensive a philosophy is, the better will it teach us the importance of previous philosophies," and there can no longer be any doubt as to the central role the history of philosophy plays in philosophy itself.

The more one reflects on these statements, the more convincing do they appear, especially in the light of the preceding study. But it also becomes quite clear, at the same time, that the basic reason why none of the proposed solutions to "the problem of the historicity of philosophy" is entirely satisfactory, is because none of the philosophers considered here has quite succeeded in framing the problem correctly.

It is a familiar maxim, in science and philosophy, that the exact formulation of a problem is half the battle toward its solution; and contrariwise, that inability to solve a problem that has long defied all efforts to that end, is strong evidence that the problem has not been correctly formulated. And instead of any of the formulations, explicit or implicit, in terms of which the philosophers included in this study have attempted to solve the problem, the correct formulation now at long last can be seen to be: *How, when it is construed as an integral part of philosophy in general, no more and no less, is the history of philosophy possible?*

Each phrase of this formulation is equally important. "An integral part of philosophy in general," means that it will not do to interpret the history of philosophy merely as a foretaste, an anticipation, of any one present-day philosophical system or theory, much less as mainly a series of errors now at long last exposed for what they are, in the light of the allegedly "one true philosophy." Rather, the philosophies of the past must be regarded as the common heritage of all present systems and theories, however antithetical to each other these systems and theories may be, and however much they may profess to reject that heritage. As indicated earlier, no man can think as he will, regardless of all the thinking that has gone before, but must do his thinking in the context of past and present thoughts which he owes to others and from which he takes his start, either by way of opposition to, or by the development of those thoughts.

"No more and no less" means on the one hand that the history of philosophy cannot of itself be anything more than history, cannot supplant the rethinking of that history in the light of present-day problems and developments; and, above all, present-day philosophy cannot be completely absorbed, as the "methodological moment," or otherwise, in past history. And, on the other hand, the historical course of philosophical speculation must be freely accepted for what it is, namely the concentrated exemplification or expression of the wisdom of all past ages. In short, and ideally, the history of philosophy should function as the fully mastered background in the light of which to wrestle with the problems of the present.

Thus the solution to this problem will reveal, at one and the same time, something of the utmost importance concerning both the nature of philosophy and the import of its history. And the thesis to be advanced is, that the solution involves a conception of dialectic, though not in the exact sense in which that conception has been employed by earlier thinkers. But it will be recalled that Renouvier, Dilthey, Bergson and Jaspers, as well as Hegel, made some use of the concept, each in his own way; and even in the "strain" which Collingwood attributed to constellations of presuppositions, as he called them, the same notion seems to be involved. Of course the place accorded to dialectic, and the meaning ascribed to it, varied from thinker to thinker, but the very recognition of a feature of the history of philosophy for which no more appropriate term could be found, by so large a number of different thinkers, surely is of itself very significant. But what dialectic means, as used in the present context, will only become evident as the exposition proceeds.

In the first place, one of the most obvious characteristics of philosophy's history is a quasi-logical rhythm from age to age, complicated and obscured though this rhythm may be, by theories which do not fit into it, or which transcend it, and so on. One might cite as a familiar example of this rhythm the current prominence given to analysis in some quarters, in exact opposition to the synthetic tendencies prevalent a generation earlier in those same quarters. Although, in each case, there are also theories which do not partake of the tendencies in question, no one can be so blind as not to recognize those tendencies very readily. (Readers will recall Bergson's account of the "no" followed by the "yes," of creative thinkers, in their attempts to give expression to the richer truth, inherent, as they see it, in their own insights into the nature of things.)

Nor is it any wonder that the richness and diversity of philosophical theories cannot be entirely embraced within some sort of formula or law such as those proposed by Comte and Hegel. This diversity, and the general reasons for it, are, or should be, too well known to require illustration here. After all, philosophical speculation does not take place in a vacuum, or even in the stratosphere, though some critics sometimes mistakenly allege this defect against metaphysics—themselves being, of course, unwitting practitioners of metaphysics, often of a dogmatic sort.

No—the context of philosophy is, as everyone is aware, one of infinite complexity, with only a part or portion of it philosophical in the strict sense of the word. There is not a significant movement, tendency, or development in science, in art, in religion, or in social affairs, which does not exert a more or less potent influence on philosophical thinking from age to age. And in addition to all this stimulus to diversity there is, as Dilthey, Jaspers and others have well observed, the additional stimulus due to the personality of the philosopher; however subtle, however opaque to the curiosity of the professional psychologist, this personal factor may be, it is obviously influential in the formation of a thinker's theories, be those theories ever so "impersonal" and "objective" to superficial inspection.

Now because of this loosely rhythmical factor, and because of this diversity in the course of philosophy's history, there exists a marked difference with the history of science, and on this basis scientists and others often proceed to cast aspersions upon philosophy and to accuse it of lack of progress such as that which marks the triumphant march of science, and in general to point to what they regard as a serious defect in philosophy. And even an occasional philosopher (*e.g.,* Bertrand Russell) will concur in this verdict.

How is the philosopher to respond to these reproaches and these criticisms? Perhaps it may turn out to be the case that in philosophy as elsewhere the best sort of defense is offense! What, for example, if philosophers were to respond to this sort of critical comment, not by deploring the failure of philosophy to measure up to the standards set by science, but by claiming the right to construe and evaluate the history of philosophy in terms of standards inherent in and appropriate to philosophy? At the very least, this tactic certainly could enlist the support of other types of history—the history of art, of religion, of political and social institutions, for example.

There are, no doubt, respects in which philosophy resembles science rather closely and significantly. For example, both science and philosophy are, or tend to be systematic, so that just as one speaks of physical science as a systematic body of knowledge about the physical world, so one refers to the philosophies of a Thomas Aquinas or a Spinoza as philosophical systems.

And another respect in which philosophy, whether systematic or otherwise, and science agree, though the plain implications of this common feature are frequently overlooked, is embodied in the assertion that there can be no finality in science or philosophy. The very idea that there is such a thing as the history of science or the history of philosophy rules out the possibility of finality in either of these fields entirely. Hence the very idea that there are any such absolute termini either of philosophical speculation or of scientific knowledge as indubitable first principles, self-evident intuitions, or atomic or any other kind of sheer factuality, is an intellectual will-o-the-wisp of the first order. In Bergsonian terms, a completed system would be only an artificial "play of ideas," not a philosophy or a science in real and intimate contact with temporal human experience. Meanings change so inevitably that even when verbal formulations seem permanently fixed, as in the case of certain logical principles, perhaps, how those verbal formulations are construed and understood changes with the inevitable new developments in science and philosophy. Moreover, and to be perfectly honest, it must be admitted that every scientific and philosophical system or theory contains within its four corners germs or elements of absurdity or irrationality. In these fields, as in all others, the ideal goal of immaculate perfection lies forever beyond the reach of all but the gods!

There is, however, along with these respects in which the histories of science and philosophy teach the same lesson, at least one respect in which they most significantly differ; and this, incidentally, is a respect in which a system of philosophy resembles a great work of art,[1] rather than a system of scientific knowledge. (This point is important, among other reasons, because it marks a distinction between the Hegelian conception of "development" and the conception of dialectic being gradually formulated here.)

Scientific systems of knowledge are regularly superseded by the further advances in the science in question (much in the Hegelian sense of *aufgehoben*); they are, as it were, completely absorbed by the next basic advance in science. To such an extent is this true, that the practicing scientist need know only the immediately preceding stages of the history of science, in order to carry on his day-by-day work intelligently. Great philosophical systems of the past, on the contrary, like great works of art, are of permanent worth and significance.[2] Like a great artistic masterpiece, the philosophical masterpieces have something to offer to every age, and to every philosopher, whatever the relations of those masterpieces to his own philosophy may be; they are literally inexhaustible and irreplaceable. It is indeed, mainly to these great philosophical masterpieces, along with the great works of art, that later generations owe their understanding of past ages, and hence come to a better understanding of their own age.

True, contemporary students of philosophy discuss and criticize an Aristotle, a Spinoza, a Hume or a Kant, in much the same way as they discuss and criticize their contemporaries—that is, in the context of present-day issues, problems, terminology, and concepts. And how easy it appears to be to measure the shortcomings, to "refute," or at least vastly to improve upon their productions! Hume's philosophical heart was in the right place, he was as good an empiricist as he knew how to be; his only fault, according to J. S. Mill, was that he was not empiricist enough; and according to John Dewey, in turn, the same criticism applies to Mill. Or Spinoza was a God-intoxicated man, indeed; but unfortunately he was absurdly enamored of geometry. And so forth, and so forth.

No doubt such critical evaluations of one's intellectual forebears are legitimate and even necessary for some valid and specific purposes. And just so, be it noted, the literary critic deals with a Dickens or a Balzac, and an art critic with a Michael Angelo. But surely, in the one case as in the other, this is not the whole story. If it were allowed to be, it would be to lay violent hands, often unworthy hands, upon something sublime in the thought of a Spinoza (or in a great novel), something so noble and so lofty that it challenges us across the ages to lift ourselves, if only for a moment, to a level of humanity and of thought far above that of our ordinary lives. That is the true Spinoza, an eternal and precious possession, in spite of all the critical strictures that may be levelled against almost every detail of his system. Like the King, Spinoza is dead; but in the former case the cry, "Long live the king," is an absolutely necessary pledge of loyalty to his successor; while in the latter case the very idea of a successor is in a very real sense out of place.

There is a sense, namely, in which no great philosopher of the past can be supplanted by any other.

And just as these Great Ones, as Jaspers appropriately and lovingly calls them, stand out from their lesser fellows, so there are certain enduring lines of thought which constitute a permanent feature of the history of philosophy, and hence, too, a feature of philosophical dialectic. A little above, reference was made to the empirical line of thought represented by the names of Hume, Mill and Dewey. One can be sure, indeed, that there will always be empiricists, mingled with other equally enduring types of philosophical theory— rationalists, formal logicians in logic, hedonists in ethics, idealists, realists, and so on.

For as the historical record clearly reveals, no amount and no potency of hostile criticism will ever permanently eliminate such persistent tendencies. When Gilson dogmatically declared[3] that the "first principles" of metaphysics are eternal, it might be said that he was simply giving expression, though in an inappropriate fashion, to the fact that there will always doubtless be adherents to the line of thought presently labelled "neo-scholasticism." And empiricism, too, will always make a strong appeal to some minds. In reply to most devastating criticisms of a Mill, a Dewey will always rise up, in some later generation, to proclaim that while valid to some extent as against Mill's particular version of the doctrine, what those criticisms really call for is not an abandonment of the doctrine as such, but simply such a reformulation and development of it as to meet those criticisms, and thus to render empiricism more truly empirical. And just so in general.

In still another way the histories of science and philosophy significantly differ. In any given period of history there are certain paramount problems which occupy much of the attention of thinkers of that period; problems which indeed often seem central or characteristic of that stage in both philosophical and scientific thinking. For science, these problems mark as it were the growing point of scientific knowledge; until they are solved there is frustration, and when they are solved, a more or less noteworthy advance takes place in the science in question. The solution becomes fully incorporated in the steadily growing body of scientific knowledge. For philosophy, on the other hand, the situation is much more complex. Rarely indeed can it lay claim to any such obvious progress; and hence the frequently voiced criticism by scientists and others, insufficiently versed in the process of philosophical thinking, that science puts philosophy to shame in this respect. But of course this criticism ignorantly measures one subject— philosophy—by standards appropriate to another— science—and thus completely fails to meet its mark. On the contrary, a good proportion, perhaps the larger proportion, of the problems which are in the forefront of the minds of most philosophers of any given age, like old soldiers, simply fade away with the passage of time, leaving scarcely a trace of their erstwhile prominence.

In the early part of the present century, for example, and more especially in the English-speaking community, one burning question was that concerning the logical status of "relations." Philosophers found themselves aligned in two dialectically opposing camps, one group maintaining that relations are logically "external" to their terms, the other group insisting that relations are intrinsically "internal" thereto. But now, in mid-century, what philosopher bestows the least attention, except perhaps by very remote indirection, on that specific question? Nevertheless, the question has neither been cleanly resolved, nor completely abandoned, but rather, gradually replaced by other questions, and transformed into other terms.

On the other hand, there are problems—again unlike those of science—that persist indefinitely and everywhere, which are ever being raised and ever being resolved anew, only to rise again, like the phoenix from its ashes, to demand a solution in the light of a new context and in terms appropriate to that context. Such, for example, is the "problem of universals."

Thus philosophical problems have a fate and an import far, far different from the characteristically successive problems of science. And all this quite apart from the point that philosophical speculation is *personal* (as explicitly noted, e.g., by Jaspers) in a sense in which science never is. For philosophy is occupied, among other things—some would hold, above all else—with values. And values essentially involve a subjective as well as an objective factor. Science, on the other hand, rightly prides itself on its impartiality, its "objectivity" (which frees it from entanglement with subjective factors, and hence from the consideration of values, though at the price of abstraction).

Finally, at many stages in history, philosophers have proposed—a proposal which would make no sense in science—an entirely fresh start either in dealing with certain issues hitherto, in their view, unduly neglected, though now at long last recognized as central to the whole subject, and revealing it in an entirely new light, or in proposing to attack old, recalcitrant problems in what seems to them a more promising way, or in some other fashion. Such thinkers are philosophical rebels, advocating a complete break with the past, and for a time they create a great stir, but eventually they quietly assume their places in the pages of history, along with all their predecessors. This, no doubt, will be the fate, for example, of the rather dreary existentialists, and of the enthusiastic advocates of linguistic analysis.

Such are some of the respects in which philosophy, in its historical dimension, displays its dialectical nature—i.e., in its loosely rhythmical, quasi-antithetical succession of philosophies, in the differences between the history of science and the history of philosophy, in the permanent worth of the great philosophies of the past, and in the persistence, through long periods of time, of various distinctive lines of thought.

That there are numerous important implications attaching to these basic features of the history of philosophy, is of course evident. And while there is neither time nor space to consider many of these implications here, there are one or two which cannot be passed over, even in a study as brief as this.

A new light is cast, for example on the diversity so characteristic both of contemporary philosophy and of philosophy in its historical dimension. Such diversities are in fact what first strike the novice in philosophy; and the "disagreement" as it is commonly called, is most disconcerting and disturbing to one who begins the study in high hopes of at last being about to grasp and comprehend "the eternal verities." And even professional philosophers, who certainly ought to know better, sometimes manifest embarrassment over what impresses them as a most unhappy state of affairs.

The late Mr. F. C. S. Schiller, for instance, once presented a paper before the Aristotelian Society with the suggestive title, "Must Philosophers Disagree?" For what was to him, evidently, a serious malady afflicting philosophy, he had, however, a simple remedy—just adopt Dr. Schiller's prescription, and all would be well. But while one may smile at the frank naiveté embodied in this prescription, one should also bear in mind that in principle it differs little from the proposals implicit in the doctrines of Gilson, Jaspers, and Russell, among others.

Agreement may sound sweeter in the ears than conformity, especially in these times when the latter is anathema to all right-thinking men in the non-communist part of the world. But what would philosophical agreement be, but conformity on the highest level, and does anyone really desire that, or conceive it to be good?

If a professor in general may be defined as "a man who thinks otherwise," how much more eminently essential this quality is to the professor of philosophy in particular! Granted that it would be well for all men to understand each other in universal brotherhood, can such understanding and brotherhood come only at the expense of sinking all differences, intellectual and spiritual? Perhaps the good old principle of unity-in-diversity has some relevance here, as in so many other contexts. At all events, unity bought at the expense of difference, of diversity in thought and idea, is a barren thing, both in life and in philosophy; and the diversity inherent in human experience, of which the diversity—the disagreement, if you will —in philosophy is but the concentrated expression, is not something to be frowned upon, but is rather to be cherished as the essential enriching element or energy of that experience. And when the dust of controversy settles, the imperishable works of outstanding philosophers invariably impress their readers as presenting a way of thinking, a way of dealing with philosophical problems, that is of permanent worth and significance. The greater the diversity of those works, the more challenging, stimulating, and enriching they are to one's own thinking.

The plain fact is, that only in and by the frank recognition and close study of the dialectical interplay of ideas, of diverse systems and theories, can one come to realize adequately what philosophy is, the enormous complexity of its problems, and the well-nigh insuperable difficulties which attend its prosecution. And what the laboratory and experimentation is to the scientist, the Socratic dialogue is to the philosopher—a necessary testing-ground for his ideas and theories, where, by discussion, by the to and fro, by the give and take, of opposing lines of thought, of different presuppositions and their implications, and so forth and so on, there gradually forms itself in his mind his own well-wrought, well-tried and well-tested theories. Is it too fanciful to look upon the whole history of philosophy as one vast, continuing Socratic dialogue, carrying out, on the grandest scale imaginable, much the same sort of discussion as those presented in Plato's immortal pages?

However that may be, it is surely abundantly evident by now that the philosopher, unlike the scientist, cannot ignore, for his immediate purposes in the present, the history of his subject. And thus it seems appropriate—partly to paraphrase a saying of one great philosopher (Kant) — to declare that philosophy without its history is blind, and that the history of philosophy, without a philosophical understanding of its dialectical nature, is just so much empty verbiage.

There are, however, features of the historical dimension of philosophy which may serve to cast some doubt, in some minds, on this conception of its dialectical nature. For example, there is the fact that it sometimes requires several philosophers to make one step in the dialectical advance of thought, thus tending to obscure, temporarily, the actuality of the advance, which only becomes evident to later generations. And on the other hand, there are instances, scattered throughout the ages, of a philosophical giant, a Plato or a Kant, equipped as it were with seven league boots, who takes several steps at once, and thus seems, at first glance, to overleap all dialectical barriers. But again the passage of time, bringing the recognition of philosophical genius to general attention, accounts satisfactorily for such an irruption in the midst of the more pedestrian developments of lesser thinkers. Again, there may be what may be called co-eval philosophies, philosophical theories which run for a time on well-nigh independent or parallel lines of development.

Of such irregularities the history of philosophy includes, no doubt, a large number. But on the other hand, it will be discovered, on closer examination, that each new philosophical theory, however wayward it may seem at first glance to the lovers of simplification, and to adherents of logical formalities, represents a genuine and at least partially successful attempt, on the part of its originator, to give expression to a portion, phase, or aspect of the struggling self-awareness of his age. For behind the individual thinker, often unduly regardless of his contemporaries and predecessors though he may be, and who may write or think with little knowledge of, or sympathy for them, there is the general bearing and interest of his age, its characteristic intellectual traits and tendencies—its *Zeitgeist,* as a Dilthey would say. And of such a thinker it can as truly be said as of one more explicitly aware of the context of his thought, that he cannot think as he may, but must think as he can, under the conditions and limitations to which all men are equally subject.

Finally, in thus calling the attention of his contemporaries to specific instances of these characteristics of philosophical speculation in all times and places, the historian of philosophy is performing an essential service. For only the history of philosophy can effectively teach the lessons implicit in this, the loosely dialectical nature of philosophy, and thus provide the necessary perspective for the critical evaluation of overly-ambitious, or one-sidedly exaggerated speculative enterprises of one's contemporaries.

But what conception of truth, it will sooner or later be asked, is implied by this dialectical view of philosophy? Every philosophical theory involves or presupposes some theory, test, criterion, or definition of truth; but the question is especially crucial, it may be urged, for this view, which may seem, rather, to lead to scepticism, so far as any *particular* theory of truth is concerned.

Fortunately, however, the answer is neither far to seek, nor unduly elaborate or abstruse. On its negative side, the implication is, indeed, that the whole truth is not to be found in any one philosophy, nor, in particular, can it be established on the basis of any simple test or criterion, or on some alleged logical or extra-logical certainty. A claim to any such effect runs counter to the very idea that philosophy does, indeed, have a history; a history, moreover, that is an integral, inexpugnable part of philosophy itself. Incidentally, every ascription of failure, such as those cited above, to some, or all, of the philosophies of the past, is based upon the mistaken notion that there is, that there must be in the very nature of the case, some such touchstone of indubitable certainty, if there is to be such a thing as philosophy at all.

On the positive side, if philosophical systems and theories are to be judged and evaluated against the background of the whole course of philosophical speculation, past and present, then this is to say that in the last analysis they must be judged in terms of their comprehensiveness and inner coherence. Every philosophy has its contribution to make, its definite role to play, in the course of the entire range of philosophy in space and time; and every philosophy reveals its defects and shortcomings, as well as its virtues, in and only in the dialectical interplay of ideas and theories of which philosophy in general is composed. In such an all-embracing context, the more comprehensive any given philosophy is—in plebian language, the more ground it covers—the greater the range and variety of the basic human problems it deals with, and the more inclusive and coherent its view of human experience—in short, the more closely the philosopher approximates to Plato's spectator of all time and all existence, the greater the claims to one's adherence that philosophy and that philosopher can command.

Finally, it is only in and by such a dialectical process as it is the thesis of this study to ascribe to philosophy, that the logical circle, to which, with Zeller's help, attention was called at the beginning, can successfully be surmounted; and the basic problem, as Professor Murphy called it, of the historicity of a philosophy which is not just simply history and nothing more, can be solved.

Truth *is* a spiritual value, as Croce, Bergson, and Jaspers, among others, fully realize.

"When all treasures are tried, Truth is the best" (Piers Plowman).

Eradicate from philosophy the respect in which it, unlike science, is personal, the "*I* cannot think otherwise," which is inherently implicit in every philosopher's work, and it would be philosophy no longer. In other words, what a man presents to the world as his philosophy, what *he* is *obliged* to think, is, in principle, no more and no less than his reading of the ultimate meaning and significance of the entire range and depth of human experience, so far as that is grasped by his thought, and formulated in the best words he can find for that purpose.

That is why philosophy, of which its history is an integral part, not only, like science, has as its main task to "satisfy the intellect" (Bradley), but also has to satisfy the whole man. In the dialectical war of philosophical ideas, and in no other sort of warfare whatsoever, every contestant is alike victor and vanquished, for all alike are animated, consciously or unconsciously, by the "intellectual love of God," and by the assurance of having attained to that "something like the truth," which as Plato long ago realized, is all that can be comprehended by mortal man. And to have attained that level of intellectual comprehension, that "intuition," is to have become the truly "free man" of Spinoza's magnificent vision.

FOOTNOTES

Chapter I

1 Ch. IV.
2 Cf. P. Bayle, *Dictionnaire historique et critique*, 1695-7.
3 Leipzig, 1742, ff.
4 7th ed., Leipzig, 1922, I. 461.
5 Cf. Ueber das Fundament des philosophischen Wissens, 1791, pp. 53-55.
6 Such is what Cousin called réaliser l'eclectisme; cf. V. Eggers, in Lalande's *Vocabulaire technique et critique de la philosophie*, 5th Ed., 1947, p. 1217, for this *précis* of Cousin's work.
7 2nd ed., Paris, 1833, sec. 4.
8 Leipzig, 1794.
9 E.g., in the latter's *Histoire comparée de l'histoire de la philosophie*, 1804.
10 Cf. his *History of Philosophy*, Eng. transl., 1891, p. 6.

Chapter II

1 Paris, 1830, ff.
2 London, 1892, transl. Haldane.
3 Ibid., p. 5.
4 Ibid., p. 16.
5 Paris, 1928-30.
6 Cf. his essay "Geschichte der philosophie" in the commemorative *Festschrift für Kuno Fischer: Die Philosophie im Beginn des Zwanzigsten Jahrhunderts*, (Heidelberg: 1907).

7 *Op. cit.,* p. 31.

8 *Ibid.,* pp. 115-116.

Chapter III

1 Paris, 1885.

2 Cf. *Esquisse,* Vol. II, p. 328.

3 *Op. cit.,* Introduction.

4 Vol. VIII, pp. 75-118.

5 New York, 1957.

6 Chapel Hill, N.C., 1954.

7 London, 1944.

8 London, 1952.

9 Cf. Bacon, *et al.,* above.

10 *Philosophy of Existence,* p. 25.

11 *Op. Cit.,* p. 27.

12 *Ibid.,* p. 28.

13 *Ibid.,* p. 29.

14 Cf. *Philosophy of Existence.*

15 *Op. cit.,* p. 44.

16 *Ibid.,* p. 47.

17 Cf. Renouvier!

18 P. 24.

19 *Essence of Philosophy,* pp. 68-74.

20 *Ibid.,* p. 41.

21 *Ibid.,* p. 46.

22 G. S., Vol. V.

23 *Ibid.,* Vol. VII, p. 222.

24 *Ibid.,* Vol. VII, pp. 290-91.

25 Cf. above, Introductory chapter.

Chapter IV

1 English Translation from the 3rd ed. by D. Ainslee, London, 1917.

2 *Logic,* p. 281.

3 Bari, 1917, Eng. transl. entitled *History, Its Theory and Practice,* by Ainslee, New York, 1921.

4 *Logic,* p. 315.

5 *Op. cit.,* p. 318.

6 *Op. cit.,* p. 323.

7 *History,* p. 158.

8 *Op. cit.,* p. viii.

9 Knox, p. x.

10 *Essay on Metaphysics,* passim.

11 *Op. cit.,* p. 60.

12 *Essay on Metaphysics,* p. 264.

13 *Op. cit.,* p. 268.

14 *Ibid.,* p. 59.

15 *Ibid.,* p. 60.

16 *Philosophical Review,* LVI, 587-592.

17 *Autobiography,* p. 97.

18 *The Idea of History,* p. 329.

19 *Ibid.,* p. 329.

20 *Ibid.,* p. 329.

21 *Ibid.,* p. 334.

22 *Essay on Metaphysics,* p. 63.

23 *Ibid.,* p. 55.

24 *Idea of History,* pp. 108-109.

Chapter V

1 Jaspers, translated in Kaufmann, *Existentialism from Dostoievsky to Sartre,* p. 23.

2 *Ibid.*

3 *Ibid.,* p. 162.

4 *Ibid.,* p. 163.

5 *Ibid.,* pp. 170ff.

6 *Ibid.,* p. 183.

7 Munich, 1957; English translation, New York, 1962.

8 Berlin, 1936.

9 Paris and Berlin, 1937.

10 Cf. Kaufmann, *op. cit.,* p. 157.

11 Edited by P. A. Schilpp, New York, 1957.

12 *Op. cit.,* p. 157.

13 Cf. Dilthey!

14 Cf. Hegel, Renouvier.

15 Cf. Royce's "blessed community."

16 Cf. Plato.

17 *Op. cit.*

Chapter VI

1 1950.
2 Paris, 1940.
3 Paris, 1952.
4 Translated in the volume entitled *The Creative Mind,* by
   Mabelle Andison, New York, 1946.
5 Eng. transl., p. 238.
6 Cf. Jaspers, *op. cit.*
7 New York, 1937.
8 *Op. cit.,* p. 318.
9 Cf. Dilthey, Croce, Collingwood.

Chapter VII

1 Cf. Croce, Bergson.
2 Cf. Jaspers, *et al.*
3 See above, ch. VI.

INDEX OF NAMES

Abelard, 100
Anaxagoras, 49
Aquinas, 100, 135
Aristotle, 49, 55, 98, 100, 137, 143

Bacon, 1, 15
Bayle, 2n
Bergson, 49, 115ff., 133, Chs. 6 & 7 notes, 149
Boutroux, 37
Bradley, 50, 149
Brehier, 28, 37, 114
Brucker, 3
Bruno, 50
Buddha, 99, 107

Collingwood, Ch. 4, 71ff., 93, 129, 133
Comte, 17ff., 31, 32, 48, 129, 134
Condillac, 4
Condorcet, 12f.
Confucius, 99
Cousin, 7ff., 15, 29
Croce, 25, Ch. 4, 79, 83, 111, 129, 149

Democritus, 48
De Gerando, 14f.
Descartes, 3, 13, 29, 98, 100, 125
Deslandes, 6
Dewey, 26, 138ff.
Diderot, 6
Dilthey, Ch. 3, 38ff., 81, 83, 101, 133

Epicurus, 49
Erdmann, 14, 29

Fichte, 43, 49, 98

Gilson, 31, 120ff., 126, 139, 143
Goclenius, 5
Gouhier, 114
Green, 50

Hamelin, 37
Hegel, Ch. 2, 31, 32f., 43, 50, 61, 68f., 72, 82, 87, 98, 100, 129, 133f., 137
Heraclitus, 50, 100
Hobbes, 3, 48
Hodges, 38, 48
Horn, 2
Hume, 48, 79, 98, 100, 138f.

Jaspers, Ch. 5, 119, 129, 133, 134, 139f., 143, 149
Jesus, 99, 105, 107

Kant, 49, 74, 79, 98, 100, 105, 109ff., 137, 145f.
Kierkegaard, 85, 87, 98, 100
Knox, 72, 76

Lao-Tse, 100
Leibniz, 6, 50, 79, 98
Lipsius, 5, 6

Maine de Biran, 49
Mill, 138, 139
Murphy, 76, 82, 114, 149

Nietzsche, 85, 87, 90, 98, 100, 105

Parmenides, 50, 100
Pascal, 98, 100
Plato, 49, 55, 98, 100, 105, 118f., 146, 148
Protagoras, 48

Reinhold, 7
Renouvier, Ch. 3, 50, 56, 60, 102, 117, 133
Rickert, 63
Russell, 123ff., 143

St. Augustine, 3, 100
Schiller, 143
Socrates, 13, 49, 98, 99, 105, 145

Spinoza, 50, 98, 100, 119, 138, 150
Sturm, 6

Tennemann, 14
Thilly, 129

Whitehead, 26
Windelband, 6, 28, 29, 63

Zeller, 20, 42, 130, 149

INDEX OF SUBJECTS

Analysis, 123, 133
Antinomies in thought, 32ff., 102f.
Art, 40-44, 65f., 119, 137
Assumptions, 73ff.

Circularity (in history of philosophy) 20, 42f
Classification (of philosophies or philosophers) 5, 14f., Ch. 3, passim, 97ff.
Communication, 103ff., 109, 111, 119
Concept (and judgment) 65ff.

Dialectic, 21ff., 27ff., 45ff., 69ff., 82, 116f., 126, 135ff.
Diversity of philosophy, 45, 40ff., 57, 93ff., 134ff., 143f.
Dogmatism, 127

Eclecticism, 5ff.
Epicureanism, 2
Existentialism, Ch. 5, passim
Experience, (Erlebniss) and history, 39ff., 54

Freedom, 33ff., 46ff.

History, 8f., 13ff., Ch. 2, 52ff., Ch. 4 passim, 92ff., 120f., 123, 128ff.

Idealism, 46ff., 83
Intuition, 115ff., 126

Judgment, logical, 65ff., 70

Metaphysics, 38ff., 50ff., 69f., 72f., 83, 121f., 132ff.
Method, 15f., 45ff., 83f., 132ff.

Naturalism, 46ff.
Neo-Platonism, 3
Neo-Scholasticism, 120ff.

Personality and philosophy, 39f., 43ff., 102ff., 111, 134
Philology, 2, 102
Philosophy, 2, 4, 22ff., 51ff., 63, 67ff., 70, 72, 79, 84, 85ff., 102ff., 111ff., 114f., 125ff., ad fin.
Platonism, 2
Positivism, Ch. 2, passim, 124f.
Presuppositions, 73ff., 81f.
Progress, 12ff., Ch. 2, passim
Psychology, 15f., 31, 34ff., 39ff., 53, 104, 122, 124f.

Rationalism, 26ff.
Relativism, historical, Ch. 3, 70, 81ff., 128
Religion, 39f., 63, 99, 111f.
Romanticism, (and history) Ch. 2, passim, 64

Scepticism, 1ff., 22, 39, 44, 53, 128f., 147
Science, (and scientists) 4f., 21f., 38, 51f., 63, 90f., 96ff., 100, 104, 123f., 135ff.
Sociology, 31ff.
Sciences, humanistic, 38ff.

Stoicism, 2
Syncretism, 5, 10
System, philosophical, etc., 21ff., 41ff.

Thought, philosophical, 22ff.
Truth, indubitable, etc., 4, 8, 19, 21ff., 68ff., 74f., 87ff., 91, 97, 105ff., 116, 147f.

Values, 68, 99ff., 111, 137ff.

Weltanschauung, (world-view) 41ff.

Zeitgeist, 25, 146